BRITAIN DISCOVERS HERSELF

First published 1950

PRINTED AND MADE IN GREAT BRITAIN BY
THE ALCUIN PRESS, WELWYN GARDEN CITY
FOR CHRISTOPHER JOHNSON PUBLISHERS LTD.
109 GREAT RUSSELL STREET, LONDON, W.C.1

DENYS VAL BAKER

BRITAIN
DISCOVERS
HERSELF

CHRISTOPHER JOHNSON

LONDON

By the same author:

CONTENTS

ILLUSTRATIONS

*The publishers are indebted to the following for permission to reproduce
certain of the illustrations: The Amersham Repertory Theatre Company, The
Bournemouth Municipal Orchestra, Mr. John Harris, and the British Travel
and Holidays Association.*

THE REGIONAL RENAISSANCE

THE regional renaissance has developed un-ostentatiously. Most of the "isms" so popular to-day require for their stimulation the constant beating of the drum plus a regular flourish of trumpets. Regionalism has slipped into usage quite without premeditation: a trend that has developed, rather than a force that has been applied. Plans and programmes are announced by the Communist Party, the Conservative Party, the Labour Party, and so on—but there is no similar announcement from a Regional Party. How could there be? For the essence of regional-ism is de-centralization, independence, self-determination; on-the-spot decisions, personal responsibility and action.

Such qualities cannot be prepared at some central office, like medicine, and handed out with the weekly rations. They either exist or they do not, in most cases according to the environment. It is no accident that the most sturdy and independent sections of the British people are often those whose circumstances place them as far as possible from the dampening effects of central control. Unfortunately in recent years there have been vast movements towards a standardization of peoples, as well as products: a standardization sometimes direct, more often subtly indirect (i.e. the commercial manipulation of the public's taste in songs and dance music which results in the same synthetic composition being whistled everywhere from Land's End to John o' Groats). This standardization was undoubtedly beginning to weaken the whole structure of British life, and if allowed to continue unchecked might well reduce this nation to a regiment of identity cards and ration books.

Many would say that this very trend still persists to-day, but I believe that the impact of the experiences of the war and post-war years has set in motion a silent revolution of the British people against the threats of centralization and standardization. This revolution might be described as a regional renaissance, or revival. It manifests itself not so much in the material sphere as in those less tangible fields termed loosely as culture and social relations. Its importance is, for that reason, all the greater. While English butter may be important to a man he can at a pinch exist on imported Danish butter or even American margarine. But he cannot expect to live for any length of time on imported ideas and standardized conceptions and at the same time preserve his own personality. All over the world this is being proved, in the constant striving of small nations to maintain their integrity and nationhood, despite the fact that some form of amalgamation might be greatly to their advantage. Even in America and Russia, the two leading countries in the world to-day, the rulers are forced to grant a great deal of autonomy within the state—(notably in Russia, where the Soviet state is in fact made up of a number of independent nations, each with its own government and culture). If the structure of other countries is examined, the same divisions will be found—France with its provinces and its sub-nation, Brittany; Belgium; Switzerland; Greece; Yugoslavia; even the newer countries like Australia—all are composed of the many variegated parts, to each of which a great deal of freedom of expression has to be allowed. Where it is not allowed, almost inevitably there is strife and unrest.

The truth is, of course, that regionalism is as old as the hills in practice, and not so very young in theory. The world began on a regional basis, and no matter how fast jet planes are able to rush over land and sea, the world must live on a regional basis or die. In the last century or so, due to industrialism and a wave of political "isms", people were beginning to lose sight of this truth. It is often the case that we tend suddenly to want that which we are in danger of losing. That is one of the simplest reasons behind the new swing back to regionalism. The avalanche of propaganda for nationalization and internationalization, mass movements, totalitarian utopias, One World, and all that sort of thing, has overshot the mark. Its appeal has been greater to people's stomachs than to their eyes. They will eat out of the same shaped tins, but they have a pretty strong disinclination to thinking according to the same textbooks. Colour, variety, disagreements; different languages, different music, different art—just as all the planning experts move into action for the obliteration of these minor obstructions, the despised ordinary people have begun to defend the doomed objects. This defence is expressed valiantly but helplessly, when some local shopkeeper stages a sit-down strike in defiance of the compulsory destruction of his life's work under some remote Ministry's order for road widening. It is also expressed, this time with triumphant success, when the people of a region refuse to bow down to the musical overlordship of London orchestras, but set to and build up their own symphony orchestra—and one good enough to come and play in London (i.e. the Yorkshire Symphony Orchestra, and the Bournemouth Municipal Orchestra).

Britain's national strength and prosperity has, in fact, been built up by its regions. Until the advent of the steam engine, life in Britain was really very much a segregated affair. People lived, worked and developed their social interests area by area, village by village. It was a very sound structure upon which to build a great Empire. The men of Britain of those days, whatever the level of their intelligence or manners, were *responsible* men. They had to be. They had to dig their own land, grow their own food, constantly to make their own decisions. If they felt some principle to be at stake, they were prepared to fight for it themselves. In this respect it is difficult not to feel that they showed some superiority to their fellows of to-day who frequently lack the courage to stand up for their civic rights and yet at the same time allow themselves to be marshalled for slaughtering in some war waged by power politicians who sit at home making pious declarations.

The Briton of old was the regional man. He knew no grey and smoky cities, paved with mythical gold. He did know his own home, his own village, his own locality; where to find food, how to build a home, how to create the necessary conditions of existence. Above all he knew personally the people of his locality, with whom he lived, worked and played. He was not, as so often his successor has become to-day, an anonymous flat-dweller among a colony of anonymous flat-dwellers, living in secretive worlds, seldom knowing one another's names. He did not, as to-day most of us do, depend on some remote monopoly for the provision of a synthetic form of heating—he went out and chopped wood and made his own fire. In the earliest days, instead of eating his frozen Argentine beef, and opening his can of carrots, he went hunting for his food. And if he wanted to entertain himself or his friends, he did not switch a button or put on a gramophone record—he stood up and sang himself, or joined with others in dancing around a fire, or maybe a pagan god.

Of course, the good old days were often bad old days, and I have deliberately stressed one aspect only. There must have been many people who suffered and starved in ways that would not be tolerated to-day. But the point I seek to emphasize remains valid. There was a responsibility for actions, if only because there was no alternative.

In recent years the world had reached a stage where this personal responsibility was almost entirely being shelved. It may be argued that the reasons for these were political, that people had been deprived of their freedom to be responsible. This is surely an evasion of the issue. Life has to be lived; Time does not wait for the subtle and slow processes of political change to unravel themselves. It may be that political ideas and planning direct the course of our lives, but we know from our own experience that—in the sense of to-day and to-morrow, this week and next—it becomes necessary to take direct action to accept personal responsibility, if life is to proceed satisfactorily. Life has, in fact, not proceeded satisfactorily for some time, and the failure must be due to our personal inadequacies as much as to any abstract political mistakes.

The last war, with all its gigantic chaos, did temporarily halt this process of avoiding responsibility. In many ways, for whatever misguided reasons, people were put into positions where they had to accept their responsibilities. The same conditions have carried into the post-war era. And so we have the United Nations and other well-meaning humanitarian efforts to produce order out of chaos. And so, under the umbrella of these various efforts nationalism and regionalism begin to fulfil their proper functions. And so, in Britain, people tire of travelling to London for their culture, desiring instead to recapture that rhythm of hundreds of years ago, when the peoples made their own cultures, on the spot.

It may be that in the international sphere the reaction against unification has come too late, that the world must sooner or later grow into one or two—ultimately, surely, one—great organization. This need not be a tragedy by any means, so long as the roots of that organization continue to spread out in dozens of different directions. There are two kinds of internationalism: that of the mass society adhering to a single unifying outlook, producing cultural regimentation and uniformity—and the more elastic internationalism, reflected at its best in some of the smaller heterogeneous nations like Switzerland, where the many parts constitute the harmonious whole. A true international culture will derive its inspiration and its power to unify by increasing the understanding of one race of the culture of another, through the contribution of regional and national cultures, opening out new vistas and showing up the small things in the life of a country which really count for so much. When Blake wrote about seeing the world in a grain of sand, he might well have been describing the importance of regionalism, which is nothing less than a localized interpretation of the universal life.

What is of first importance in any structure is not the top floor, but the basement. Internationalism is the top floor of our house, and nationalism is the ground floor. But under the ground floor lies the basement, and if that is faulty the whole house may collapse. Regionalism forms the basement of our society to-day. It may be very tempting, for many reasons, to block up the stairs and pretend there is no basement— but the rot will not be long in making itself felt. Far better to open up the basement, to make sure of its strength and reliability, before attempting to build the house further.

Analogies are never very fair, always rather

too easy to strike. But I would suggest that the recent trend of events, in Britain at least, provides material for a very good case of regionalism. And the main argument I would put forward is the simple fact that the trend has been quite spontaneous. At the risk of repeating myself, I would emphasize that nobody has "taken up" regionalism. No political party, so far as I am aware, has specifically preached regionalism as part of its policy. The regional renaissance has arisen in Britain because our peoples are not prepared to be organized into cypherhood. The British are a nation, and like all nations they are simply a conglomeration of smaller nations, themselves a further conglomeration of regions. There is really no such thing as a Britisher— there are Welshmen, Scotsmen, Irishmen, Northerners, West-countrymen, Midlanders, East Anglians, Cornishmen, and so on. Each reflects a way of life, a cultural background, which we would be ill advised to exchange for greyhound racing, the Sunday newspapers and Hollywood films. In the hope that the British people are well aware of the folly of so doing, I offer the following brief but encouraging outline of activities in the new, and let us hope, permanent regional renaissance.

LITERATURE

THE regional writer, and regional literary activities in general, form the backbone of English literature. Their history stretches a long way back, much further than that of the sophisticated court poets and satirists—back, in fact to the beginning of time, when primitive tribal man used to tell, sing or dance the story of his adventures, around a fire at the entrance to his cave. Looking back on the main body of English writing we cannot fail to be impressed with the consistent way in which its roots are buried in the solid earth of regional life. From Defoe to Jane Austen, Fielding to Walter Scott, Dickens to Thackeray, Charlotte Brontë to Mrs. Gaskell— reading the work of any of these great writers one is conscious of how much of its quality depends upon its regionality in conception. For Dickens and Defoe the region was London; for Scott the Highlands and Lowlands of Scotland; for Thackeray the red-sanded fields of Widdicombe and for the Brontës the wild wind-blown heights of Haworth Moor. How *could* Emily Brontë have written *Wuthering Heights* if she had lived in Bloomsbury? Equally, how could Dickens have written *Oliver Twist* if he had spent his life on a

Scottish croft? Each writer—each artist, musician, dancer, each and every one of us as individuals—must have a narrowly confined background, a native, familiar surround, from which, directly or indirectly, he can draw the inspiration for his work. The criticism that this local inspiration may outwardly be almost unexpressed is nothing but a red herring. To take a modern example, Dylan Thomas, regarded by many as a poet of genius, writes metaphysical poetry—but he is Welsh-born, Welsh-reared, and his Celticism runs like fire through his work, shaping its greatness.

To-day although the nature of modern development has concentrated most publishing activities in the metropolis, a large part of modern English writing remains regional in its background. During the 'twenties and 'thirties there developed a cult of the sophisticated, satirical writers—Huxley, Waugh, Greene and their influence remains. Graham Greene, least regional of all our writers, is probably to-day the greatest living English writer. But against those few names, it is possible to range a string of other important ones: Rhys Davies, Sean O'Casey, Frank O'Connor, Gwyn Jones, Liam O'Flaherty, Mary Lavin, Hugh MacDiarmid, Fred Urquhart, James Bridie, Edwin Muir, Margiad Jones, Sean O'Faolain, Naomi Mitchison, A. L. Rowse, Phyllis Bentley, Eden Philpotts. Every one of these writers reflects the literature of a particular region, Wales, Scotland, Ireland, the North Midlands, the West. This, by the way, is not to imply any limitation upon them as writers. Our whole national culture takes its shape and force from the different kinds of writing produced by writers living and observing in different parts of the country.

The position has been put very well by E. W. Martin, writing on "The Necessity of Regionalism" in *Voices*:

"Regionalism is a necessity in any culture . . . . It is a cultural effort which attempts to endow a specific region with all that is unconsciously its own. The artist must look at Sussex, Devon or Cornwall to see it as it is; to give the half-buried lore and custom a true shape and reproduce the spirit of the area. This may be called semi-fascist idealism; but surely if we aim at a new foresight such idealism may be used with caution so that it does not atrophy into sentiment or nonsense. Restrained patriotism, a natural love of a known area, can generate forces that will produce art. Much of our literature has sprung from this response to beauty and tradition. The other element, the one which must loom over regionalism and which transcends all boundaries is the international or universal culture. The one could not exist without the other."

That is why I would emphasize how mistaken those critics are who (almost automatically) make a condescending approach to the regional writer, as if the aura of "provincialism" is indicative of his inferior quality. Rhys Davies or Frank O'Connor may write what seems a simple tale of village life in their native countries—but examined more closely the tale will often be found to possess a universality beyond the achievement of most of their urban contemporaries. There is, indeed, a strength and a neutral poetry about the work of our Celtic writers which seems to give them an enormous advantage in power over the more heterogeneous English writers. Some of the most interesting developments in regional writing of the past few years have, in fact, come from Wales, Scotland and Ireland. This is not surprising, for they have the advantage over other areas of Britain that as well as being regions they have maintained their sense of nationhood. Thus, in Wales, despite the swamping of the country with English influences, there is to-day a most vital national literature in the works of the late Caradoc Evans, Rhys Davies, Gwyn Jones, Kate Roberts, the late T. Rowland Hughes, Glyn Jones, T. Gwyn Jones, Saunders Lewis, Wynn Griffiths, Dylan Thomas, Vernon Watkins, Margiad Evans, Eiluned Lewis, Keidrych Rhys, George Ewart Evans and others. Most of these, though Welsh-born and Welsh-speaking themselves, have written and achieved their reputations in English. There is, however, a large group of Welsh-speaking and writing authors, headed by Kate Roberts and Saunders Lewis, and recently deprived by death of its two shining lights, the late T. Rowland Hughes and the late T. Gwyn Jones. Rowland Hughes was perhaps the best example of a purely Welsh contemporary writer. His first novel, *From Hand to Hand*, caused a great stir in Wales when it appeared in 1943, and sold 10,000 copies—a remarkable figure for a book printed in Welsh (though it should be remembered that at the last census, nearly a million Welsh people still spoke Welsh). Before his untimely death in 1949 Rowland Hughes wrote four more novels, all in Welsh. He was also a poet, and twice won the bardic chair at the National Eisteddfod of Wales. His work, like that of Kate Roberts, presents an unforgettable picture of the Welsh quarrymen and their world—a picture that could hardly be achieved so directly in English.

Nevertheless, Welsh writers are turning more and more to a language which can reach them a much larger public. One reason is the obvious economic one: namely, that if they are to reach a wide enough public to enable them to keep on writing, their work must be presented in English. Another, more idealistic reason, is a desire to educate the English people into a greater understanding of Welsh ways of life, outlook and character. But whatever the reasons the emergence of an Anglo-Welsh literature, largely replacing

21

the previous Welsh-speaking literature (now confined to the National Eisteddfod and a few privately sponsored publications) does suggest that English will ultimately become the main literary language of Wales. In some ways this is a loss to regionalism; or, more correctly, to nationalism. But in practice, I feel the result has been almost the reverse. To take a sporting analogy, the Welsh writers have learned English and proceeded to beat the English writers in their own language. The consequence has been a strengthening of confidence among the Welsh in their own native talents, and a much greater respect and admiration from the English.

The same sort of trend can be traced in Eire, a country with a vital native culture—but, unfortunately, outside the scope of this book. Ulster too, has produced a crop of important new writers since 1939—notably Michael McLaverty, John Hewitt, Roy McFadden, Robert Greacen, W. R. Rodgers. The latter once wrote of his native land:

Bearnagh and Lamigan and Chimney Rock,
Spelga, Pulgrave and Cove—all these names
   lie
Silently in my grass-grown memory,
Each one bright and steady as a frog's eye;
But touch it and it leaps, leaps like a bead
Of mercury that breaks and scatters

Suddenly in a thousand shining strings
And running spools and ever-dwindling rings
Round the mind's bowl, till at last all drop
Lumped and leaden again to one full stop.

This passionate love of country seems to achieve intensity among the writers of small countries. It is particularly noticeable among the Scottish writers, whose voices have been heard in increasing volume in recent years. Hugh MacDiarmid is the best known of the Scottish nationalist writers, and he has inspired many other younger writers, like Sydney Goodsir Smith, Douglas Young, Maurice Lindsay, Adam Drinnan, Hamish Henderson. James Bridie is perhaps Scotland's best-known writer, at least in the theatrical field, along with novelists Eric Linklater, Naomi Mitchison and Neil Gunn. A good deal of Scottish writing has tended to overdo the nationalist approach, to the extent that the propaganda comes first, the art after (a fault of much of MacDiarmid's work). A better balance between the two has been revealed in the work of a young writer, Fred Urquhart. His first novel, *Time Will Knit*, is one of the few genuine proletarian novels of our time. Unlike so many pseudo-proletarian writers—or, equally bad, working men who cannot write but will attempt to do so on the theory that the writing of a plumber is bound to be interesting because he is a plumber—Urquhart both derives from a working-class background, understands it from within and without, and is at the same time a professional writer with an improving gift for dialogue. It is by dialogue, largely, that he captures the inimitable Scottish way of speaking, and the character of the Scottish working people. Reading one of his novels is like entering a Scottish family's house and sharing their lives. No greater tribute could be paid to a regional writer.

In Wales, Scotland and Northern Ireland, three areas which I have briefly touched upon, the wartime years and the subsequent period have witnessed a much greater awakening of the peoples to the importance of preserving their national cultures. The same upsurge of native pride has been witnessed in the various regions of Britain—notably in the West Country, one-time province of Thomas Hardy, R. D. Blackmore and "Q", more recently of the Powys brothers, Henry Williamson, A. L. Rowse and others. Whole books have been written about the Powys brothers, so I can hardly compress their background into this short article. The most purely regional of them is T. F. Powys, author of *Mr. Weston's Good Wine* and other books certain to be classics of the future. Louis Marlow, a great personal friend of Powys, once remarked that he was a truly West Country writer because he drew his original inspiration from the soil of Dorset and, mystic that he was, breathed into his characters a breath which was life on the earthly and the divine plane. What he meant, and it is true of all the Powys brothers, is that they transform what is local and regional into the universal realm. Another West Country writer, A. L. Rowse, is best known as a poet, but one of his most significant achievements was his autobiographical *A Cornish Childhood*, with its detailed description of village life and of the author's struggle to rise to academic as well as literary eminence. In the past two years we have had yet another example of the emergence of a Cornish regional writer—Jack R. Clemo, a young Cornishman in his early thirties who was recently the recipient of an Atlantic Award. Born the son of an illiterate clay worker, Clemo has lived all his life in the same tiny Cornish village of St. Stephen, and for much of that time he has suffered from semi-blindness and total deafness. The amazing thing is that despite these handicaps he has taught himself the art of writing to such good effect that his *Wilding Graft* was acclaimed by the leading critics as a first novel of great significance. In his second book, an autobiography, *Confession of a Rebel*, Clemo gives a fascinating picture of his development among the weird surroundings of the clay pits. He also describes with insight and sympathy the life of the local people, lived out in

25

a curious muddle of stark realism and inherent mysticism. Above all, Clemo manages to convey something of the grey that is essentially Cornwall, grey granite and grey seas—toughness and passion. Reviewing a book of Clemo's the *Cornish Review* suggested that at last Cornwall, the real Cornwall, had found its own contemporary novelist. Which means when expanded—as in the words of Howard Spring, who wrote "of all the English fiction published this year I was most held by *Wilding Graft*"—that another name must be added to the list of regional writers of national importance.

It is possible to find examples from other regions of Britain. I do not know of another Arnold Bennett emerging from the Midlands, but from the north there is the very encouraging case of Sid Chaplin, a former miner, born and bred in a Northumberland village. A complement, at the other end of England, to Jack Clemo, he also is a young working-class writer, imbued with a religious fervour, with a natural gift for describing and interpreting the local life around him. Where Clemo has written novels, Chaplin has concentrated largely on short stories, and it was a book of his short stories that won him an Atlantic Award. Chaplin is a better craftsman than Clemo; on the other hand, he lacks the power of the Cornishman's clumsy, burning passion. Both, however, are triumphantly original in lifting up out of obscurity the life of their regions, painting it without falseness, re-creating it with integrity in words.

Other regional novelists who have attracted national attention include Graham Sutton, with his trilogy of life in the Cumberland fells; R. H. Mottram and Neil Bell with their stories of life in East Anglia; and T. Thompson, with his Lancashire dialect stories. Then there have been a large number of writers who prefer to make their approach mostly through non-fiction; John Moore author of *Portrait of Elmbury* and other pictures of Gloucestershire life; the farming writers, A. G. Street and Adrian Bell; poets like A. L. Rowse of Cornwall and Norman Nicholson of Northumberland. The wireless, too, has given an opportunity for many literary men to create something new in the way of regional literature—i.e. John Betjeman and his delightful descriptions of country excursions.

Perhaps the most varied and significant focus for the work of regional writers, however, is represented by the many regional literary magazines, nearly all of which have appeared during the past ten or twelve years. It may seem curious, or even suspicious, that so many of these reviews have appeared at the same time. Is it a cult? A new fashion? I do not think so. The same conditions that are bringing about the general revolution in our ways of life and behaviour have encouraged the development of these magazines. The war, throwing people back upon their own resources, at the same time released a wave of creativeness. The widespread desire to write has continued, and exists among a larger section of the population than ever before. This, and the fact that some national literary papers have died out and the survivors are space-hungry is one of the main factors behind the development of so many regional publications. There is also the matter of a revived pride in native localities, which sets up a protective rearguard action against the massive world tendencies towards an urbanized centralization.

The process is a happy spiral. A writer or group of writers embark upon a regional venture, discovering what an enormous scope for writing is offered by local life and culture. Other writers and artists observe and add their contributions—amateurs, too, encouraged by the visible evidence, try their hand, and practice is a good taskmaster. Gradually a new reading public is formed, and a living organism is built up. It may, as with all ventures, collapse, but at least local writers and readers receive a welcome tonic.

The regional literary magazines of the British Isles have developed in two groups: the national magazines of Wales, Scotland, Northern Ireland and Eire, and the county or provincial town literary reviews. The first group came first. Such

publications as the *Dublin Magazine* date back to
the 1920's, while *Wales* and *Welsh Review* both
originated before the Second World War, as did
Voice of Scotland. Another excellent Eire review,
The Bell, ran through the war years and after-
wards, though it has recently stopped publication.
These and other regional publications have in
their time been able to publish regularly the work
of such established writers as Sean O'Casey, Sean
O'Faolain, Mary Lavin, Frank O'Connor, Liam
O'Flaherty, Rhys Davies, Gwyn Jones, Dylan
Thomas, Vernon Watkins, Glyn Jones, Margiad
Evans, Hugh MacDiarmid, Fred Urquhart,
James Bridie, Edwin Muir, Naomi Mitchison.
If only for this reason, they have been outstanding
among the little reviews appearing in Britain
during the past twelve or fifteen years. At a time
when many London reviews were arising and
disappearing, these papers were playing a vital
part in a very real renaissance of their country's
literature. As far as possible, too, the reviews of
all three nations have endeavoured to nurse a
number of young writers into maturity. *Wales*
and the *Welsh Review* were of great value to the
development of Dylan Thomas, Glyn Jones, Emyr
Humphreys, Keidrych Rhys, Vernon Watkins
(and, most notably, the late Alun Lewis). The
Voice of Scotland provided Hugh MacDiarmid
with an outlet denied him by many other reviews
and *Poetry Scotland* gave encouragement at the

right time to a promising school of younger Scottish poets.

The purely regional papers have been able to offer more scope to lesser known writers. In many cases such magazines have been launched by groups of writers, largely as a vehicle for their own work—i.e. *Bristol Packet*, organ of the Bristol Writers' and Artists' Association (now defunct); and *Exe*, the quarterly organ of the University of the South-west at Exeter.

Invariably, regional reviews reflect an emphasis in one way or another typical of their background. *Mercury*, a new Bournemouth review, gives a great deal of space to music because the town has many flourishing musical activities and a first-class symphony orchestra. *Chelsea*, as might be expected, breathes a strong flavour of painting and painters (though it has wider ambitions!—claiming "What Chelsea thinks and does in the sphere of the Five Arts is the only thing worth doing and thinking and the rest of the world should know about it"). The *New Shetlander*, published from Lerwick, is devoted largely to articles about island life and culture, with notes on wild life and old crafts. Most regional reviews rightly attach much importance to the continuation and revival of local crafts.

Other features common to these regional reviews are biographical studies of famous men and women of the locality, archaeological and industrial surveys, reviews of drama, music, art, and books by local artists and writers, and poetry and short stories of local interest. While naturally this type of very local review has fewer well-known writers to draw upon for contributions, mention might be made of the following reviews and contributors: *Northern Review* (Phyllis Bentley, Sid Chaplin, Graham Sutton, Henry Moore), *West Country Magazine* (Jan Stewer, Eden Philpotts, Geoffrey Grigson, John Arlott, John Betjeman, Anne Treneer), *Cornish Review* (Ronald Bottrall, Francis Bellerby, R. Glynn Grylls, A. L. Rowse, Ronald Duncan, A. K. Hamilton Jenkins), *New Shetlander* (Naomi Mitchison, Seton Gordon, Richard Perry), *Chelsea* (William Kean Seymour, Ursula Bloom, Arnold L. Haskell), *Writers of the Midlands* (Leslie Halward, John Hampson, Edward Galbraith).

I cannot speak for other editors, but being the founder and editor of a regional review myself, the *Cornish Review*, I can say from experience that the regional literary magazine has a most important function in the life of the community. In Cornwall, for instance, there had been no county review since "Q's" *Cornish Magazine*, of fifty years ago. Yet the county is, and has for a long time, been teeming with cultural activities that go far beyond the scope of the county's several excellent local newspapers. No sooner was the *Cornish Review* announced than editorial material and annual subscriptions began flowing in, thus evidencing the need for such a publication. With such a wealth of editorial and artistic talent available, as in Cornwall, an editor's task is much simplified. At the same time I believe he should have a precise conception of the sort of material he wants, aiming constantly at interpreting the culture of the locality in every possible direction. For that reason the *Cornish Review* prints a series of articles on their work by craftsmen living in the county, also a series of written portraits of Cornish towns and biographical studies of writers and artists of Cornwall; while a number of special surveys of industrial and cultural trends are regular features, since the two are very much interwoven in the life of the county.

Perhaps in Cornwall there is a special advantage in dealing with an area that is a cultural unit, in some ways a smaller Wales. But I am sure that every English county, and many English towns or industrial areas, could well sustain a literary review of their own. Judging by the present trend, this is not an ideal beyond accomplishment. The result, giving encouragement to a much wider range of young writers, might well be an ultimate enrichment to British literature as a whole.

So far I have dealt with regional literature from the point of view of writers and writing. Equally interesting has been the development

THE BRAEMAR GAMES

H. R. H. PRINCESS ELIZABETH AT THE NATIONAL EISTEDDFOD OF WALES

on the other side of the fence, among the reading public. It is a truism now to remark that the war, involving for hundreds of thousands of people many long hours of solitude, brought an increase in the reading of books. That trend has continued, fostered partly by publishers, partly by libraries. The chairman of the Public Libraries Committee of the Borough of St. Pancras once said that if the Public Libraries of the borough were to be effective they ought to be considered the spearhead of local culture. There was a time when few public libraries could have qualified for such a compliment, but in recent years libraries all over the country have made enormous improvements to their systems and scope. A typical provincial library to-day, quite apart from the basic service for which it was originally designed, will also offer its "customers", lectures, discussion groups, exhibitions. In the regions, many libraries now operate mobile library vans that travel out into the countryside, calling at one village after another.

The work of the libraries has been greatly encouraged and stimulated by the National Book League, a comparatively new organization sponsored by publishers, booksellers, authors and members of the public. The League has opened branches in many parts of the country, and these organize frequent meetings and lectures. Typical of the varied programmes organized by the

C

League are the following: "Putting into Print" Exhibition at the Castle Museum, Norwich; a Children's Book Week at Barnet, Herts, Library; a lecture by Ivor Brown on "The Man Shakespeare" at the Culverden House Adult Education Centre, Tunbridge Wells, Kent; a talk by Chester Wilmot of the B.B.C. at High Wycombe. The League publishes a lively magazine of its own, *Books*, containing articles on every aspect of reading, in books, and altogether has done a great deal all over the country to stimulate local interest in reading.

Many organizations now exist to encourage appreciation of literature in the regions. Writers' clubs are to be found in every town in England from Perth to Penzance. Prominent amongst these are the Writers' Circles who have their Annual Summer School at Swanwick, Derbyshire. Then there are organizations such as the Association of Yorkshire Bookmen, with the aim "to foster a love of books". The Leeds branch recently sponsored a lecture session which included F. Austin Hyde on "Yorkshire Dialect and its Humour"; Sid Chaplin, the Durham writer, on "The Short Story"; James R. Gregson, former Drama Director of the B.B.C. North Regional, on "A Dramatist's Notebook"; L. A. G. Strong on "Poetry in the Modern World"; A. A. Thomson on "The Anatomy of Humour"; and Margery Sharp on how she dramatized her novel, *The Nutmeg*

34

Tree. Visits were arranged to the Stratford-on-Avon Theatre and the Brontë country.

Many poetry societies have been built up in recent years, and one that has an especially strong regional background is the new British Poetry Association, whose aim is to encourage the appreciation, study and development of poetry. The Association's journal, *Poetry*, states. "Towards this end it will foster regional activities and looks to enthusiasts throughout the country to establish regional groups. A panel of lecturers and readers has been drawn up, for visiting branches. Public and private meetings, competitions, festivals, sponsoring publication of poets' work (when finance permits) the selection of a 'Book of the Year', close contact with the Commonwealth and foreign countries through liaison officers—all these are developments on which the Association is working. Their realization would make the British Poetry Association unique in the world."

I would not like to conclude this brief survey of regional literature without drawing attention to the strong literary aspects of many provincial newspapers. There are some local papers that are heavy and stodgy, but it is surprising also how many others there are that manage to accommodate in their pages a great deal of literary matter. This is particularly so in areas with a strong literary tradition, such as Yorkshire, the

Lake District, Wales, Cornwall, Hampshire and the East Coast. Many papers in these areas—the *Cornishman, Montgomery Times, Petersfield Advertiser, Yorkshire Post*, are but four examples—will devote a considerable amount of space to book reviews, interviews with local authors and other subjects of literary interest.

Quite apart from their literary aspect, these local newspapers contribute very strongly to the regional revival by their steadfast refusal to be swamped by London ways and fashions. W. L. Andrews, editor of the *Yorkshire Post*, recently wrote in the *Northern Review* that provincial newspapers were not poor relations of the great papers printed in and around Fleet Street, but different, "far more neighbourly".

"The Royal Commission does not seem to have given a great deal of attention to our provincial weekly papers. Why should it? There is little to be said against them. They serve their communities well. Think of the general outlook of a weekly paper editor in Yorkshire or Lancashire. He cannot walk down the High Street of his own town without being saluted and buttonholed. Somebody with a long face stops him to say, 'That report of poor old Bill Smith's funeral that you printed was all wrong. You had the names of all the other members of the Old Codgers' Bowling Club but you never mentioned me.' Somebody else makes him smile again by saying, 'Thanks very much for that report of the annual meeting of our Clough End Allotment Society. It's bound to do us a power of good.' Then somebody stops him to ask if he has heard that burglars got into the house next door to the Police Station and snaffled Mrs. Whatsit's new fur coat—the one her husband gave her for her silver wedding. When the editor goes to the 'White Swan' for a drink and then lunch, you may be sure that aldermen and councillors will pull his leg about the prim stickiness or the wild you-be-damnedness of his latest leader.

"What is the effect of this daily neighbourly pressure, reinforced by letters from readers telling of mistakes in the paper—for all of which the editor is blamed? He is kept under a wholesome discipline by his public, and is bound to be zealous for accuracy and proportion. He insists on careful reporting, and his leaders and notes reflect editorial steadiness."

Something of the same might be said of regional writing. It is writing that is curiously intimate and specific, because the writer is among his material. By studying a single area, or a single group of people, regional writers are able to achieve a penetration and grasp of life that is missed by many less rooted writers. Furthermore, as they become more familiar with their material, so they gain confidence.

Think of old William Barnes of Dorset, the

dialect poet of whom Llewellyn Powys once wrote, describing a visit to Barnes' grave at Winterborne Came:

"No poet in all English literature has done more to reveal the quality of homely village days as they follow one after the other, against their background of the fugitive recurring season. These bucolic poems, so innocent and so sturdy, instruct us how to become accessible to the wonder latent in every mode of natural existence, teach us to be grateful for the privilege of life in its simplest terms, with firm purpose and serene minds, to face our inevitable lot of sorrow and death."

No writer could ask for a higher tribute. And it applies to many more regional writers, without whose work British, or any other literature, would be aimless and anaemic.

ART

THE artist is the least responsive to any national trend towards urbanization and centralization. He must have the freedom to wander, to seek out ideas and inspiration, to meet new people and places, to widen the scope of his experience and understanding. He may live among the massive distractions of a city, but will take good care to see that he escapes into the horizon beyond as many times as possible. There is something of a myth in the saying that London or Paris are the centres of their nations' art activity. These two cities are the places in which are centralized facilities for training in art, for meeting other artists and exchanging ideas, for seeing exhibitions of the world's best work, and so on. But it is surprising to study the actual work produced by artists living in these centres and to find what a large proportion of it is about, or inspired by, some far-away subject—a country river, the wild coast of Cornwall, a Mediterranean village, peasants in the mountains, dancing in a Spanish square, climbing in Switzerland, a lake in Ireland. This tendency applies even to abstract paintings, many of whose creators will testify that in order to create they have to be in a certain place or atmosphere—say by the sea, or up in the mountains—even though their surroundings are not directly reflected in the resulting picture. Thus it is not unfair to suggest that our great art of to-day, as in the past, is largely regional in context. Just as John Constable spent most of his residential life in London, but for his great works of art went again and again back to his beloved Suffolk countryside, so, to-day, to take a contemporary example, a leading painter like Stanley Spencer returns again and again to what he once described quite seriously as his "kingdom of heaven", Cookham churchyard, for inspiration and, often subject. Looking at the matter from these two quite different angles we can see that, in general, the artist will tend to turn from city to provinces in his attempts to capture beauty in his art.

This is not really so surprising as it sounds. London is, after all, merely one place—the rest of Britain is a million-and-one places, containing within them the most diverse elements of life and appearance. Inevitably, the one offers the artist a greater challenge and wider scope than the other. I say, in general, because naturally there are some artists who work better confined within the noise and bustle of a city. Artists who are gifted in that way follow their instincts and may well produce great art (a contemporary example might be L. S. Lowry, the Manchester painter).

But it is interesting to note that very often this sort of painter concentrates upon people, the person, the individual, often portraying a condition of hardship and suffering. In the city the individual must tend to become a cog, a part of a machine—and so the city artist is forced to dramatize and emphasize that very part of him, the human side, that is in fact slowly being crushed. In the regional areas, particularly the predominating one of the countryside, the individual is less of a machine. Consequently the artist is very often less concerned with the individual, more with the whole pattern of life, the flow of the season, the growth of crops and animals and the place of the individual in that rhythm.

Each of these approaches to art is equally valid and sincere; but the first is a recent development, the product of our modern civilization, whereas the second has been a natural part of artistic tradition since the beginning of time. To-day the modernist and abstract artists are in the ascendancy, and rightly so, because this is a time of change, revolution and upheaval. It is a time of near-chaos, and if artists are to reflect and represent the world around them, they must find ways of doing so that are applicable. Then again, the position of the artist in society has changed. From being a decorative and aesthetic influence, he has tended to become a prophet and an oracle (not always, unfortunately, to his own advantage). It is difficult to judge the work of Picasso, Klee, Dali and other moderns without having regard to its political and moral purpose. No such conditional approach was necessary for judging the paintings of Constable, Gainsborough, Wilson. Like artists in other fields, the modern painter has been forced out of his own little world. Even if he follows the apparently detached profession of painting pretty flowers, all the significance in the world attaches to the style in which he paints the flowers. If he paints them in one way he may be looked on as little more than a photographer; if he paints them in the opposite, symbolical or even abstract way, he may be expressing all sorts of messages and psychological attitudes. If I make this sound slightly humorous, I must apologize, for it is really a serious point. As with many other facets of life, the scope of art has widened and deepened, into spheres previously unsuspected. It is all the more important, then, to try and judge art not by former standards, nor by any single standard—rather to approach it tolerantly, even humbly, seeking to find out its basic quality.

Such is a necessary background to any consideration of the development of regional art in Britain. Great artists are rare events, and I would not suggest that regional Britain has produced an unusual number of great artists in recent years (in the sense that regional writing has). What has taken place, however, is an event of equal importance. That event has been, simply, the artistic awakening of the people of Britain. It is the old story, following the same pattern as other arts—that which was once the rich man's exclusive pursuit at last becoming available to everyone. But the story of art is a little different from literature and music, both of which can be made available, through books, concerts and the radio, to millions of people. We have not yet, unhappily, reached the stage where people, as a whole, either want or are able to adorn the walls of their homes with original paintings. On the other hand there is no doubt that such will be the ultimate results of the new awakening of the British people to the value of creative fine arts, as represented by painting, carving, sculpting, etc.

As in the theatre and music, this development of regional interest in art has sprung out of the upheaval of the war, the encouragement of the Arts Council and the activities of local groups of enthusiasts. In the chapter on regional theatre I emphasize that the part played in that sphere by the Arts Council is relatively a small one, that the major effort has come through individual local initiative. In the field of art I think it is only fair to pay a tribute to the work done by the Arts Council as a spearhead of the drive to produce a more enlightened attitude towards art. This work has, and rightly, been concentrated almost entirely on the regions. Its nature has been twofold. In the first place the Arts Council has sent out regular exhibitions on outstanding works of international art, giving millions of provincial dwellers their first introduction to the full impact of the rich colour and draughtsman-ship of the masters. Secondly, wherever possible, the Council has endeavoured to facilitate ex-hibitions of work by local artists, or groups of artists, either by direct subsidy or partial subsidy.

The only real criticism of this first aspect of Arts Council encouragement is that there are not enough of these international exhibitions. Most of these, including as they do many famous and priceless pictures, can only be shown in a limited number of large towns and cities. All over Britain local arts clubs and societies organize parties and hire motor coaches, often travelling long distances in order that they should take advantage of the chance (perhaps of a lifetime) to see original paintings, like the Van Gogh show, the paintings of the Italian Renaissance, or Goya and other Spanish masterpieces. Returning to their own groups and localities, they bring back and pass on through debates and discussions, a wider appreciation of the art of genius.

In its ventures into the local type of exhibition, the Arts Council has been rather more discreet, perhaps over-cautious. Where money is the sole obstacle to the production of an exhibition of work by a local artist or artists, it is very tempting to demand, "Why on earth can't the Arts Council put it on?" The fact is, Arts Council funds are public funds and have to be accounted for very carefully. In the long run, though, it is extraordinary how this obvious fact is overlooked: the money it spends is our money, yours and mine, gathered in taxes of one sort and another. There are many powerful opinions ranged against the work and existence of such bodies as the Arts Council—another reason to encourage a certain caution. In general, the Arts Council has followed a middle course, an example being its recent participation in an exhibition of the paintings of Alfred Stevens, the Dorset painter, at Blandford Arts Club, Dorset. Here the exhibition was guaranteed against financial loss jointly by the Arts Council and the Dorset County Council. In Guernsey, in the Channel Islands, the States Council provided the money to buy the buildings for an arts club, and the work of reconditioning was made possible by a grant made through the Arts Council, added to the local efforts of the Guernsey Guild of Arts. In other instances the Arts Council has provided complete models and plans for arts centres, which have been adapted and applied by local councils (i.e. Mablethorpe and Sutton-on-Sea, Newcastle-under-Lyme, Plymouth, Bridgwater). The now customary, and most satisfactory method for sponsoring civic arts centres seems to be for the financial burden to be shared between local art lovers, the local authority and the Arts Council. The prestige of the Arts Council is now such that its favourable opinion will often influence a local authority. One West of England Town Council now devotes a $1\frac{1}{2}d$. rate to an arts centre and some of the more expensive entertainments held there. Many others, like York, have undertaken the praiseworthy task of altering and improving their public art galleries, introducing better lighting, more colour furnishing and surrounds. Still more encouraging is the news of many councils opening new galleries. Just after the war the Scarborough Corporation had the foresight to acquire a lovely Georgian house, commanding a fine view of the sea and gardens, and open it as the town's art gallery. Another north country town, Batley, has recently opened a new art gallery whose policy is essentially a progressive one. Temporary exhibitions of paintings are shown in the gallery as often as possible and emphasis is on the smaller good exhibitions rather than on the larger and perhaps only mediocre collections. "The gallery is contemporary in its outlook and encouragement is given to the living artist rather than to the artists of the past centuries." A worthy sentiment, borne out by the fact that among painters represented at the first exhibition were such modern painters as John Piper, John Tunnard, Ivon Hitchens, Graham Sutherland, Henry Moore and David Homberg. At Netherton the council have made their library-by-day into an arts-centre-by-evening—at Swindon the town's art gallery is similarly used for meetings and discussions at night. In many areas towns are co-operating to share exhibitions—i.e. in South Wales, in Wessex, and in the north of England (where some fine pioneering work has been done by the Temple Newsome Gallery at Leeds, home of Henry Moore).

This form of regional co-operation is having excellent results and is increasing. Thus, in the north, for some years there had been in existence numerous art societies, each doing a good job on its own, yet none of them large enough to feel able to embark on more ambitious projects. Recently ten of these societies got together and formed the Federation of Northern Art Societies with the following constitution:

> To arrange for closer contacts between clubs in order that they could exchange ideas; and for the promotion of their practical interest.
> To seek to raise the general standard of art and its appreciation in the area.
> To encourage and assist the formation of new clubs.
> To keep clubs informed of art activities in the district.

47

To hold an annual conference and a combined annual exhibition.

To encourage the idea and formation of similar federations in other parts of the country; and ultimately the formation of a National Federation.

Following its formation the Federation inaugurated an annual exhibition, held at the Shipley Art Gallery, Gateshead, at which more than 200 paintings were hung, in club groups. A Federation Bulletin is published quarterly giving news of local exhibitions, etc., and the Federation co-operates with the Council for Arts, Music and Drama in Northumberland, in the organization of week-end schools, tutored by such painters as Barnett Freedman, Michael Rothenstein and William Coldstream.

In studying some of the northern regional publications, papers like the *Northern Review* and the *Northerner*, sponsored by the King's College University of Durham, one sees at once from the numerous reproductions of paintings that there is a real revival of painting in the north. Perhaps on a still more notable scale have been the recent developments in the very westernmost tip of Britain. Cornwall is, perhaps, a special case, since it has been associated with painting for many years, and is well known as the home of several art colonies (apart from Chelsea, the only official art colonies in Britain). Many artists, from

PLYMOUTH ARTS CENTRE

THE NATIONAL LIBRARY OF WALES, ABERYSTWYTH

Whistler to Sickert, Munnings to Ben Nicholson, have been drawn to Cornwall, as if pulled by some sort of magnetic force, and on them all the curiously elemental character of the place has exerted its influence, directly or secretly. An excellent imaginative interpretation of how Cornwall affects the artist has been given by a young sculptor of St. Ives, Sven Berlin:

"The open coliseum of each little cove of sand and of rock may be the theatre for any natural, supernatural or unnatural event. The unending presence of the sea breathing ceaselessly over the shoulder of each hill, the rock charged with a thousand sunsets or carved by a hundred years of rain, the little trees loaded with berries growing away from the prevailing wind, offering crimson to green, the mind's incessant vertigo at the cliff-edge, and the slow constructional flight of the seagull—these things in some way act as the chanting of magicians and open up the deeper rooms of experience in man, make him aware of his being part of the natural universe at the head of a great unseen procession of dogs and devils, spectres and dragons; of being a channel for unknown and undefined forces; of facing the mystery of life, awakening powers of perception which search behind the frontiers of normal events . . . ."

Since the end of the war there has been a widespread revival of the Cornish art colonies, and

D

to-day there are several hundreds of painters working, mostly down at the western tip, but many also at Looe and Polperro, Mevagissey, St. Mawes and Falmouth. Large societies of artists exist in East Cornwall, Falmouth, Newlyn and St. Ives, with their own regular exhibitions, galleries, etc. The most recent of these to be formed, and perhaps the most stimulating as an example of truly regional art development, is the Penwith Society of Arts in Cornwall. Formed by a group of progressive and abstract artists, the new Society took over an old hall, converted it into a modern well-lighted gallery, and there presented its first show in the spring of 1949. What has made the Penwith Society such a novel development is the fact that its membership, and exhibits, represent the work both of artists *and* craftsmen. So the visitor to the Penwith Gallery is greeted not only by a tasteful, and somewhat provocative display of paintings, ranging from the abstracts of Ben Nicholson to the traditional work of the Society's chairman, Leonard Fuller— but also by a large exhibition of pottery, printing, furniture, embroidery, wrought iron and other Cornish crafts.

The Penwith Society claims that in this respect it is unique in Britain, and there is no doubt that the experiment is proving a successful one, for after only one year the Society was able to report numerous sales. It is, of course, fortunate in

having some of the leading artists and craftsmen in Britain among its members—such as Ben
Nicholson; Barbara Hepworth, sculptor; Bernard
Leach, potter; Guido Morris, printer; A. Carne,
maker of wrought iron. There is probably no
other area in Britain so intensively alive with
working artists of one sort or another. So perhaps
if the Penwith experiment were tried elsewhere
(if it were possible to try it, so much of its success
being bound up with the atmosphere and way of
life in Cornwall) the same success might not be
obtained, if only for lack of outstanding artists.
Nevertheless, I would recommend to other regions
the serious consideration of similar exhibitions,
which combine much more than just painting—
crafts of all sorts, as well as debates, films, etc.—
and which can achieve a wholeness and roundness
of purpose lacking in an exhibition confined to
paintings. Especially is this sort of exhibition
valuable to a region, which is reflected in particular through its traditional crafts.

Cornwall is of course only a small corner of
Britain, and in other aspects of the regional problems might not merit such special mention. But
in the field of art it lies well to the forefront, and
provides a very suitable example by which other
regions might measure their own achievements.
For one of the effects of so many artists residing
in Cornwall has been to make the county as a
whole art-conscious, to the extent that original

paintings are to be found hanging on the walls not only of numerous private houses, but (in St. Ives at any rate) in almost every café, hotel and public house. The effect of this extra-penetration of art into everyday life of the people is in all ways a good one, and of course is how art should operate, a part of the natural order of things.

Scotland and Wales are two other regions where art has flourished in recent years. Scotland, notably, has produced a number of the more gifted of the younger painters, men like Robert Colquhoun and Robert MacBryde—and the country is reasonably well provided with exhibition centres at Glasgow, Edinburgh, Dundee, Perth, Aberdeen, etc. There are several organizing bodies, like the Royal Scottish Academy, the Society of Scottish Artists and the Fine Art Society of Edinburgh. Rather more interesting has been the development in Wales, a country hitherto badly served in the art sphere. There is much to be done, of course, in Wales. One of the official organizers of art in Wales, David Bell, has written in the *Welsh Review*:

"The task of distributing art exhibitions widely in Wales lies in a practically virgin field. The reasons why religious, educational, and most cultural institutions in Wales have cultivated other arts than the fine arts, which have played only a very small part in Welsh life, are not hard to find. For one thing, the nature of Welsh society which was formerly so diffuse and poor in urban centres, and, more recently in the industrial south, so lacking in any tradition rooted in the local life, has not been able to provide that wealth and sophistication in which the arts are most often found to flourish. In the past the fine arts were the monopoly of a section of society which exists in Wales only in isolation from Welsh national life, and in circumstances which are foreign to Welsh institutions. As a consequence of this, little provision for the public exhibition and enjoyment of works of art has at any time been made, and Welsh people who are keenly alive to musical and literary enjoyment, are educated in musical and literary taste, are often lacking in any understanding of past or contemporary art, such as the exhibition of pictures to advantage must presuppose. The problem, therefore, is twofold; on the one hand to find adequate accommodation for exhibitions, and on the other to choose pictures for exhibition which will have some significance where they are shown."

After that somewhat gloomy prospect it is heartening to learn that the Arts Council exhibitions are now regularly touring North and South Wales. In one period no fewer than eleven separate exhibitions were sent to eighteen centres. One of the most successful of these was a show of the work of Josef Herman, a Polish artist who

settled in a tiny Welsh mining village, Ystradgyn-
lais, in 1944, and has remained there ever since,
painting the miners and the life of the village.
This has been an interesting case of an artist with
a European background and training, entering
into the closed circle of Welsh village life, being
accepted by the people (who talk of him as "Joe-
bach"), and succeeding in finding a way—through
pastel paintings—of bringing out all the richness
and intensity of that hard life of the Welsh miner.

Some of the exhibitions brought famous European paintings to the Welsh people, but many
others concentrated on the work of Welsh painters
like Augustus John, Wyndham Lewis, Gwen John,
Cedric Morris, David Jones.   In addition, the
South Wales Group, a new body formed by the
combined art societies, amateur and professional,
working in conjunction with the art schools, has
sent on tour an exhibition presenting the best new
Welsh paintings. The Contemporary Art Society
for Wales and the Arts and Crafts Section of the
National Eisteddfod (of which I write more fully
in another chapter) have also sponsored shows
and competitions. The feature of these, and of
much of the art activity in Wales, is the predomi-
nance and promise of the amateur painters. This
was recently reflected in a show of children's
work sent on a tour of all Welsh Art Clubs, also
in another exhibition of thirty drawings and
paintings entitled "Some pictures from a South

Wales Town". This was arranged from work by members of the Merthyr Tydfil Art Society, and consisted of paintings by adults and children who are not themselves professional artists. In this sense it represented a departure from the normal policy of the Arts Council, and was intended rather to encourage the development elsewhere of such groups of "Sunday Painters", working together on the possible lines, than to demonstrate a standard of achievement. The exhibits showed great vitality and individuality, and were yet another testimonial to the fact that at least in this age we are more appreciative of the potential gift of the artist in every child.

Another sort of regional exhibition that has proved remarkably successful has been that which achieves a living presentation of local arts and crafts. For instance, the Isle of Purbeck Arts Club, Dorset, recently arranged a complete exhibition around the work of artists in the famous Purbeck stone. Members of the Ancient Order of Purbeck Marblers attended the exhibition and carried out work on their crafts, while two local sculptors—Elizabeth Muntz and Mary Spencer Watson—also came along and worked on pieces of sculpture in the local materials. Writing of the exhibition a local paper commented on the keen interest that it aroused from the crowds who came thronging every day.

"It was fascinating and heartening to watch

boys and girls working away happily with the tools of the marblers, and achieving most creditable first attempts. Perhaps a few of them will have come to the conclusion that, after all, there are more rewarding ways of life than driving a lorry. If they do, for that reason alone the exhibition will have been triumphantly worth while."

It is not possible in a book as short as this to go into great detail, otherwise it would be fascinating to consider many other facets of the art situation—how, for instance, in many provincial towns art school students are going round their local schools painting murals on the walls. Then again, some of the more progressive industrial concerns in the Midlands and north of England are now employing artists to paint pictures for permanent hanging in factory canteens, clubrooms and institutes. One of the big Scottish shipping lines follows a policy of buying original modern paintings by younger artists for hanging on its steamers.

The church, alas, has not been very much to the fore—the famous Burghclere Murals, in which Stanley Spencer executed at a little chapel at Burghclere in Berkshire, were privately commissioned. How paltry this attitude seems compared to Europe, where there is more than one case of a local church and its community commissioning first-class artists to execute new religious paintings and murals in the church. Some years ago a venture of this nature was embarked on by Father Bernard Walke, instigator of the famous St. Hilary Nativity Plays Broadcasts, when he persuaded notable British painters to paint panels for his lovely old Norman church of St. Hilary, Cornwall. The panels are still to be seen, and looking at them it is difficult not to feel a stir of excitement at the thought of what could be done in the churches all over Britain, if only every little community would set out to revitalize its church with new and colourful design paintings, murals and other artistic decorations, using wherever possible the services of local artists.

Perhaps, too, one day in the not too distant future we shall witness teams of artists falling upon ugly eyesores and turning them into things of beauty, with a rapidity such as Nature could not rival. At any rate, the progress is in the right direction, for attendances and attitudes at Britain's hundreds of art and technical art colleges have expanded immensely in recent years. At almost any art school courses can now be taken in painting, sculpting, engraving, modelling, carving, as well as the art-craft sections of pottery, woodwork, printing, etc. The fact that there is really not much more hope for a rosy future for the professional painter to-day than in the past (for the Arts Council has merely replaced the old patron, and its financial help is limited) does not seem to deter more and more people from turning to art. Money, fortunately, is not always the aim of artists, who regret its absence far less than the opportunity for their pictures to be of service to the community. All over the country now through thriving sketch clubs and art societies, schools and art groups, paintings are passing into the everyday currency of life. Soon they will be, let us hope, as natural as books or gramophone records. Some towns, indeed, are already investigating the possibility of lending out original paintings. In Leeds the City Gallery now lends out paintings to local factories for exhibition to workers. At one time Wakefield Art Gallery had a system whereby subscribers to its Permanent Art Fund could borrow pictures. Something on these lines, considerably intensified until it approaches the public library system with books, is an ideal worth aiming at all over the country. Nowhere will it be more welcome than among the peoples of regional Britain, with their newly awakened thirst for good art.

THEATRE

IN no sphere is the regional revival more vividly illustrated than in that of the theatre. The days when the word theatre really meant the West End of London seem a long way away now. The London theatres continue to offer some of the best of modern drama, of course. But what has happened out in the smoky wilderness of those previously despised provinces? What is stirring down the long lanes and among the far-flung villages of rural England? (and Wales, Scotland and Ireland for that matter).

The answer, in brief, is that the theatre has at last gone out to meet the people. It began, as did much of the new regional revival, during the recent war. This is no reflection on the many pioneering developments of pre-war days, the Liverpool Playhouse, Birmingham Repertory, Cambridge Festival Theatre and so on. They were the pioneers whose efforts showed the way. They propagated an idea, or rather an ideal, which always had to struggle hard for existence. It always will, of course—but now there is no longer that deadening feeling of its being a losing struggle. Culture, whatever Lord Beaverbrook and others may say about it, has at last become

59

recognized in Britain as a valuable product, worth cultivating. And the theatre is one of its most tangible aspects.

This was recognized during the war years, when the air raids on London and other big cities put a premium on theatrical performances, while at the same time the large-scale redistribution of the population created swollen populations in areas without adequate theatres. As is so often the case where there is a threat of deprivation, people suddenly become aware how much they wanted that which they might lose. They began to take action, forming new dramatic societies and theatre clubs, setting up committees, converting halls. At the same time, thanks to the enthusiasm of the late Lord Keynes, the Government was persuaded to set up the Council for the Encouragement of Music and the Arts (now the Arts Council).

So the regional revival of the theatre began to take shape. The C.E.M.A. sent the Pilgrim Players and other groups on tours of areas, many parts of which had never seen professional theatre before. Regular visits were organized to factory hostels in the Midlands, the North, South Wales and Home Counties. Before the end of the war more than 100 of these hostels were being visited regularly, each having built or converted its own theatre. Considerable publicity was given at the time to the tours of these industrial areas by large companies headed by such stars as Sybil Thorndike and Lewis Casson. It should be remembered that they were complemented by regular tours undertaken by local repertory companies. Very often these tours involved playing every night at a different town or hostel, and this might mean long journeys, perhaps in the depth of winter, in an open truck or an over-crowded theatre van. Conditions varied too. One company that made Merthyr Tydfil its main centre and played a ten weeks' tour of the surrounding South Wales mining areas, found itself playing one night in a huge modern hall of the Miners Welfare Association holding 4,000—the next in a village hall with seating for less than 100. But the warm and enthusiastic audiences, and a sense of real appreciation, made all the hardship worth while.

That has been the keynote of the revival of the regional theatre. Plays of the calibre of *Hedda Gabler*, *Twelfth Night*, *She Stoops to Conquer*, *Arms and the Man*, *The Importance of Being Earnest*, are taken to the four corners of Britain and welcomed. We hear of *Major Barbara* being performed at Tenby and *Playboy of the Western World* at Milford Haven in both cases by the Western Players under the sponsorship of enthusiastic and energetic local arts clubs. The Arts Council has continued not only to sponsor provincial tours but to subsidize permanent regional companies. An example of this latter policy was

61

provided in West Yorkshire, where the West Riding Theatre was set up, consisting of three interchangeable companies based at Halifax, Huddersfield and Wakefield. At Bristol and Salisbury the Arts Theatre has acquired its own permanent theatres, and the Council has also facilitated such ventures as the experimental Company of Four, playing at the Lyric Theatre, Hammersmith, and at Bristol, Cambridge, Brighton and Cardiff.

But the initiative, financial and moral, given by the Arts Council, is only one aspect of the regional revival of interest in good theatre. The financial help is only partial, and the success or failure of repertory companies depends finally on the amount of local support, of which there has been a steady increase. There has been a widespread increase in the number of repertory theatres launched, and it has been estimated that there are now more than 200 repertories in Britain and Northern Ireland. In some cases the sponsors have been over-optimistic, and after a season or two the theatre has had to disband. Such setbacks are inevitable and they do not alter the main picture, one of an ever-increasing penetration of local repertory into the natural and cultural life of Britain.

Almost any one of the repertory companies has a fascinating story to tell. Here there is only space to take one, and hope that it may serve as a sample of all. Early in 1947 a group of young actors and actresses formed the Studio Players of Camborne, in Cornwall, and took over the lease of a derelict hotel. For five months they worked between themselves, converting the hotel into a modern little theatre, seating nearly 200. In the words of their leader, Victor Thompson:

"The dirt and squalor surpassed imagination. The garage, now the main foyer, was piled high with cinders and debris, the doors broken. The old stairway to the ballroom was all but impass-able. Rain-water had turned the refuse lying in the corridors into a morass of pulp and filth so deep that it was practically impossible to gain access from the main buildings into the ballroom. To this, through the ragged gaps in blackout boards, came the last flickers of daylight. Here amidst the flotsam and jetsam left by successive occupation of troops, firemen and Services' canteens, we deposited our chattels. . . .

"The remains of cottages on one boundary were pulled down, holes gaped in the ballroom walls, panelling was ripped down and the building seemed, if possible, even more derelict than before our occupation. Late one evening we began to remove the floorboards of the ballroom and within ten days the stage itself was completed. Our efforts were switched to the proscenium walls, and as these reached upwards our spirits rose. As the weeks passed, the café and foyer, box office and staircases took on their rough shapes, and late each night it was usually possible to surprise one or other of us pacing the bare stage looking out into the empty hall and seeing there in imagination the audiences that would one day fill our little auditorium."

Camborne, Cornwall's busiest industrial area, had never had a repertory theatre before, and there were many pessimists who predicted that it wouldn't have its new one for long. In fact, the theatre was opened by the veteran actor, Cyril Maude, in August, 1947, and has remained open ever since. Much of its success, as the company would be the first to admit, has been due to the practical help of local people; the formation of various advisory committees, and finally a Studio Playgoers' Club, that holds regular meetings to discuss future plays, as well as concerts, dances, etc. Thus the people of Camborne are able to feel that this is their local theatre, its future largely in their own hands.

Camborne's story can be repeated from all over Britain, often on a much more ambitious scale. Amersham, Guildford, High Wycombe, Petersfield, Harrogate, Perth, Dundee, Newcastle, Northampton, Oxford, Cambridge, Sheffield—these are just a few of the centres whose repertory companies, at one time or another, have made an important contribution to the development of regional drama. The common point that links so many of these regional enterprises, and gives them such a human advantage over London's West End theatres, is the co-operation between players and audience. Camborne is not the only theatre that has literally been built by the common efforts of local inhabitants who wanted to bring the drama to their town. At High Wycombe what had been an old disused swimming bath was transformed into an up-to-date little theatre, without any hired help. Supporters of the new Rugby Civic Theatre (opened at the end of 1949, the first place of live entertainment in the city for twenty years) constructed new dressing rooms, excavated space below the stage, put up a new proscenium arch and redecorated and reseated the auditorium. It must have been hard and tiring work, but the sort of work that unites and strengthens—finding practical recognition when the Rugby Borough Council promised to contribute £2,000 to pay rents and rates on the theatre for the first three years. This sort of support from local authorities is becoming much more common. The Lord Mayor of Norwich recently launched an urgent appeal for a building and endowment fund for the Maddermarket Theatre, to which, he stated, "the City of Norwich owes much of its distinction in the artistic sense in this generation". What a welcome contrast to the pre-war days when, unless there was a wealthy enthusiast ready to dip into his own

E   65

pocket, as with Sir Barry Jackson and the Birmingham Repertory Theatre, the bravest of regional ventures was likely to perish for want of l.s.d.

Whether or not there is official local support, however, it seems that the new wave of regional theatre activity cannot be suppressed. Up in Scotland the Glasgow Citizens' Theatre was founded by James Bridie in 1943, and was received so well that a grant of £1,000 offered by the Arts Council has never been drawn upon. In 1945 the Theatre moved into the Princess's Theatre, and from there aimed at presenting plays of artistic or didactic merit which would not otherwise be seen in Glasgow, "of a quality sufficient for Scottish dramatists (if any) to write up to". James Bridie himself, famous nationally and internationally as a playwright, has suggested that Scotland makes an excellent laboratory for decentralization experiments. Scotland, he says, has never been thoroughly centralized either in spirit or in fact, and it has never had a theatre of its own.

"It is a country abounding in natural drama. It dramatizes its domestic and political events from the smallest to the greatest. It has a tradition of racy, pithy expressive speech. Better still, when applying itself seriously to a venture, it is in the habit of making a kirk or a mill of it and not allowing it to dissipate in hot air."

The idea of a national theatre, still far enough away from realization in England itself, is being discussed a great deal in Wales. The precedent that is always taken as an ideal example is the Abbey Theatre of Dublin, so successful in presenting the very highest level of its nation's plays, with work by Yeats, Synge, Shaw, O'Casey and others. Nigel Heseltine, a Welsh writer who has worked with the Irish National theatre, has put forward a concrete and interesting plan for a Welsh National Theatre with two full-time companies, one of which would tour North Wales all summer, the other South Wales. In the winter the North Wales company would play at, say, Swansea, and the South Wales company would spend the season at Caernarvon. The following year the South Wales company would tour North Wales. The plan includes the setting up of a large Welsh School of the Theatre, or possibly a Stage University, and the arrangement of exchange visits with the Abbey Theatre of Eire, the Group Theatre of New York, the Compagnie des Quinze and other overseas theatres. "If enough of us want a theatre in Wales we can have it," writes Mr. Heseltine.

The same might be said about England, though tribute should be paid in passing to the Stratford Memorial Theatre, whose standards and calibre have increased tremendously in the last few years, so that each summer season at the little Warwickshire market town is an event not only of national but international importance. It is only fitting that Shakespeare's plays should be regularly performed at the town of his birth. What is needed now is that the idea should be carried further, so that in many different parts of the country theatres put on seasons of plays by native playwrights. This has been done to some extent by the Bradford Civic Theatre, with a number of plays by Yorkshire-born J. B. Priestley; and I believe the plays of Eden Philpotts are regularly featured in Devon theatres. This system could be developed as a complementary to the idea of a national theatre in London, to which would come performances of the best of these regional plays. (A successful pointer to this idea was a recent series of productions in London by four regional repertory companies, the Bristol Old Vic Company, the Liverpool Playhouse, the Birmingham and Sheffield Repertory Companies.)

Yet another example of regional theatre development has been the very considerable extension of travelling theatres. One of the principal exponents of this has been the Unity Theatre Movement, a Left-wing organization with main headquarters in London and Glasgow. While the Unity has professional companies in the cities, it has formed an affiliation of amateur companies with aims similar to its own all over the country.

There is a National Organizer employed to encourage and assist the formation of new companies as well as to be responsible for the setting up of schools for actors and producers. Unity sends companies out into suburbs and provinces, villages and other isolated parts, as well as to factory canteens and Army camps, parks and even street corners. Plays with a political message form the bulk of Unity's material, and they also encourage and finance a number of promising young playwrights.

Theatre Workshop is the title of a regional group with headquarters in the north of England, which travels from town to town in a given area. This workshop is representative of a trend towards communalism among the repertory companies, the members working as a team, sharing the off-stage donkey work as well as the acting; holding debates and discussions with playgoers, constantly focusing the attention not just on drama, but on really good and alive drama. The Adelphi Theatre Guild is another outstanding example of the travelling theatre. At different times this company has been stationed in Ireland, Cornwall, the Midlands and the north-west of England. The Compass Players and the Pilgrim Players are two further examples of groups who, like the Unity Theatres, are united in their work by a policy and ideal. These policies vary in words, but usually hold in common a determination to bring theatre off the remote and inaccessible West End floorboards, and down into the heart of the community life of the British population, area by area, town by town, village by village.

So far I have written of the professional theatre, and how it has grown in the regions as never before. Part of this success has undoubtedly been due to the co-operation, and one might well say the pre-educative work, of the amateur theatre. Just as the professional theatre has in the past tended to remain centralized in the great cities, so the amateur theatre has been at its strongest in the more remote areas. Partly, of course, because of the need to fill a gap left by the non-existence of professional theatre—but more, too, in order to provide an outlet for the natural talent of local people. This is not the place to go into a detailed history of British amateur dramatics, but their extent and ramifications is truly amazing. Anyone who may have attended, whether as player or spectator, any of the innumerable Drama Festivals held all over Britain will testify to the enthusiasm, hard work and talent to be encountered.

The trend of recent years has increased the quantity of amateur dramatics. Societies like the Bournemouth Little Theatre Club can claim a membership of more than 1,400, and this is only one random example. What is more important is the steady improvement in the *quality* of amateur acting. To a large extent this has been encouraged by the training now provided through the County Drama Organizations, whose officials not only adjudicate at local contests, but arrange schools for the training of producers and actors. Frequently these are held at large country houses, or in schools, being spread over a week, or a long week-end, thus giving people a chance to discuss their common problems.

Youth is at the forefront of the minds of County Drama Organizers, which is one reason why drama plays such an important part in the new Youth Club movement. In many counties, too, special summer youth camps are held, with drama as a main subject. An interesting example of the initiative being displayed comes from a West Country area where the Drama Organizer obtained permission from H.M. Ministry of Works to use the precincts of a famous ancient castle as an "operational base" for a week's course on drama, open to the students of a nearby international youth camp. The organizer felt, rightly enough, that the unique setting—the high circular walls of the castle set on a hill and open to the sky and surveying the countryside for miles to the distant sea—would in itself stimulate the student's imagination. Developing this line of thought she presented the students with a challenge.

"Here was a castle, apparently dead and in

71

ruins—could we, working together for a week, by means of the drama and the historical knowledge we had gained, revive the corpse? It would involve hard work—plenty of it. I had no ready-made play to put into rehearsal. We should have to create it out of the human drama known to have been enacted within the castle walls. Then I introduced them to the fact which I had discovered by chance during my own research into the history of the castle, and which was stranger than fiction. The last day of the course happened to fall on 21st August. On the morning of that very day, 304 years earlier, Sir Richard Grenville, the King's General in the West, had stormed and captured the castle from the Roundheads. Here was a stepping-off stone for our play—could we resurrect the events of that day? The idea clearly seized on the students' imagination, and during the interesting discussion that followed it was obvious that the challenge had been taken up. There and then the play was born."

From then on the group built up a play, the events of which included the presentation of "St. George and the Dragon" by Village Mummers, followed by a folk dance of the period. The play was not put into writing but was built on improvisation, and the producer found that the rehearsals showed a remarkable degree of concentration by the cast. They obviously felt that this was their own play in the making. One group of students painted the scenery, another made the costumes, others went out and spread news of the performance, which was finally held before an enormous audience, gathered from many miles around.

But the value of this example lay not only in the final performance. As the organizer wrote afterwards, it was both a stimulant to international friendship and a useful exercise in concentration. But there was something else, too. "Perhaps the best answer to the question, 'What was the value of it all?' was a remark of one of the cast, overheard after the performance: 'Well, that castle looked dead when we first saw it—now it seems so much alive that we will never forget it.' "

This concept of choosing a play with a local theme or background as the most suitable for an amateur society is spreading in the regions. The verse plays of the north-country poet Norman Nicholson have been acted in his own region by local societies, and many of the university town societies have put on plays by their own students. The extent to which this can be carried was shown when the Redruth Amateur Operatic Society hired a London West End theatre for a week in the spring of 1949, took up their players and several hundred supporters in a fleet of motor coaches, and put on a Cornish play written by the secretary of the Society and played by its members. The play was not a brilliant success,

but the enterprise at least deserves full marks—
a little more of this sort of "invasion" might be
good for London's complacency.

Some of the regional amateur societies have
sought to emulate the professional companies in
the inter-change system, and one society in the
north-west suburbs of London exchanged with a
little amateur theatre in Holland for one week of
the summer in 1948. Another scheme that has
proved highly successful has been the now well-
known "Dramatours". These originated in the
Bromley Little Theatre, Kent, where the producer, Wilson Pook, had the idea of taking the
company round the Isle of Wight holiday camps
and the R.A.F. and Army sanatoriums in Kent.
The members of the theatre made the tour their
summer holiday.

The following year Mr. Pook canvassed other
dramatic societies, and companies of eight to ten
players were formed. Rehearsals were carried out
during the spring, and then week by week the
companies were sent out on a series of one-night
stands of holiday camps. Subsequently a contract
has been made to tour the Butlin holiday camps.
Each of the companies consists of amateur
actors, spending their summer holidays doing
just what they most want to do—taking part in
live theatre before very live audiences. According
to Mr. Pook, Dramatourists come from every
walk of life, ranging from near-children to old

men of seventy. Many people split their annual holiday into two separate weeks, and go on a tour in each week. Already some of the actors and actresses have attracted professional attention but that is, generally speaking, a side issue. The bulk of the players are simply acting for the fun of it—and an excellent experience it has proved.

It is impossible even to begin to list the activities of amateur societies all over Britain, but I want to emphasize the interesting new trend, by which their services are now being made use of by local civic authorities as part of the general civic entertainments season. Thus, the Birmingham City Council engaged local societies to give plays in the Birmingham parks every Saturday evening, and another group gave an eight weeks' season of plays in a special marquee built by the Council. At the Finsbury Open Air Theatre in London, eight local societies gave a four weeks' series of performances, attended by more than 13,000 people. It is certain that this sort of cultural co-operation will be extended in the future—indeed, a feature of the 1951 Festival of Britain is the number of drama activities organized jointly by local authorities and societies. In many parts, local or county councils have sponsored contests for full-length plays for performance at the Festival. In Somerset the County Drama Committee worked out a plan to tell the story of Somerset through a series of full-length

75

plays, with material based on actual fact—the writing of the scripts being done by members of the Somerset Playwrights' Circle, and production arranged by affiliated clubs. One group at Wells has written a play about the Witch of Wookey, while another group at Minehead has written episodes in the lives of Wordsworth and Coleridge while staying in that district. From Taunton comes a play about the famous Bloody Assizes of Judge Jeffrey, and from Wincanton a play on the legend of King Arthur.

The future of regional drama in Britain will incline more and more to this sort of local development, illustrated in detail by my example about a play in the grounds of an ancient castle. Ever since the recent war broke up the centralized pattern of social life in Britain, people have become more aware of the reality of their local ways of life. Correspondingly, people in the cities have shown dissatisfaction with the comparative rootlessness of their lives, as evidenced by the applications by thousands to leave the cities and take up work on the land. Economic necessity may hold people to the cities, although a policy of regional distribution of industries may help towards rectifying this unfair bondage. Meantime, among the millions of people already living in the less crowded parts of Britain, a new pride is springing up in local activities. In the field of the drama lies one of the greatest chances

76

for focalizing and strengthening this regionalism. It is, after all, not so very many years since town guilds and other groups of players would stage local religious plays in churches and market squares, all over the country. Village mumming-plays, guise-dancing plays and other off-shoots of these events have survived to this day, particularly in those parts most distant from London— Scotland, Wales, the Isle of Man, Northern Ireland, Eire and Cornwall. Old customs die and new ones take their place, but there is no reason why the best of the old should not be absorbed into the new. Perhaps the producer had the right idea who recently formed a theatre group among the inhabitants of a tiny fishing village and persuaded the tough old fishermen and their wives to try their hand at Shakespeare, but acted in their own natural way. There is within us all a capacity for expressing ourselves in gesture and speech, and the drama has always provided a natural outlet. The tendency towards standardization of manners and voices, appearance and behaviour, so notable in the large cities, makes it all the more imperative that in the less highly organized areas of our society every attention should be given to preserving local customs and outlooks. Nothing can contribute more effectively to this end than the steady development of regional drama, presenting, wherever possible, plays by local people, acted by local people, for local people.

MUSIC

MUSIC is in many ways the most universal of all arts. As a famous conductor once said, as soon as ideas are expressed in words the possibility of misunderstanding arises, perhaps followed by arguments which may even become heated — but through music sympathetic understanding is immediately established and language barriers are broken. It must often have been the dream of great composers that their works might, in their universality, unite the peoples of the world. Music can have contributed least of all the arts to any disunity in the world. Whatever their relations in the political sphere, the peoples of Britain, Germany, Russia, America, Spain and other countries have always been sympathetic to one another's music.

An example of this was provided during the last war, when thousands of civilians and soldiers packed out the popular concerts at the Royal Albert Hall, when leading symphony orchestras played programmes by Brahms, Beethoven, Wagner and other German composers. At that time many London critics wrote, with a sort of condescending surprise, on this remarkable new interest of the man-in-the-street in music. Reports were beginning to come in of the remarkably warm receptions being given in isolated Army camps to productions of serious music, symphony concerts and instrumentalists. In fact it was really this country-wide response to good music that was the most significant development, for unlike the London boom, now languishing, the regional revival has persisted and solidified. Nevertheless, this revival owes a good deal to the London wartime concerts at which so many thousands of Service men and women from the provinces made their acquaintance with good music. When finally they returned to their home towns and villages they took with them a determination that sooner or later the same quality of music should become available in their local areas.

Miracles cannot be achieved overnight, and there must still be many areas of Britain without adequate local music facilities of first-class quality. All the same, it will probably surprise many readers to know just what has developed even since the end of the war. For example, there has been an increase in the number of provincial symphony orchestras. The most famous of them, the Hallé Orchestra of Manchester, is an old established one; its subsidy for so long by the Manchester Corporation has been a creditable case of municipal enterprise. To-day it is significant to observe how other, less concentrated areas are beginning to develop local orchestras into semi-national institutions.

Notable among these is the Bournemouth Municipal Orchestra, which was completely re-organized after the war. According to *The Times* music critic, "in a couple of years Mr. Rudolph Schwartz has brought this orchestra to a pitch of general excellence that matches the London orchestras, and a pitch of enthusiasm only found elsewhere in the Hallé". To-day the orchestra is a permanent body of seventy players, blessed with one of the finest concert halls in Britain as its residential home, the Bournemouth Winter Gardens. (This fact in itself has probably contributed greatly to the players' achievements.) A series of nearly 300 programmes have succeeded in getting away from the usual humdrum, safety-first programmes favoured by provincial orchestras of old. Thus quite apart from the favourite main symphonies, the Bournemouth Orchestra has played new works by contemporary British composers, such as Benjamin Britten, Vaughan Williams, William Walton, Edmund Rubbra, Lennox Berkeley.

At the Anniversary Concerts in 1949, the Orchestra played for the first time "Suite No. 3", specially written for the occasion by Gordon Jacob, and dedicated to Bournemouth. The concert was a civic occasion, the Mayor and other dignitaries of Bournemouth being present to

THE AMERSHAM REPERTORY THEATRE COMPANY
IN SOMERSET MAUGHAM'S "THE CIRCLE"

THE BOURNEMOUTH MUNICIPAL ORCHESTRA

celebrate something bigger than just the Bournemouth Orchestra playing on its "home ground". For the Orchestra is now beginning to serve Wessex in general, giving regular concerts at Portsmouth, Southampton and other centres. It has even, and quite confidently, taken London by storm, giving concerts at the Royal Albert Hall—what's more, getting receptions as enthusiastic as any London orchestra.

Bournemouth must be an unusual town musically, for in addition to its own Symphony Orchestra, it has a Municipal Choir, a Chamber Music Society, and a Wessex Opera Company, which it is hoped will one day become the Bournemouth Municipal Company. Indeed, Hampshire as a whole is musically very active, having its own County Music Committee which "shall concern itself with the encouragement of music in the county and to this end shall co-operate with the Musical Education Committee of the Carnegie United Kingdom Trust in the administration of funds. It shall further concern itself with the co-ordination of all musical activities in the county". The committee has its own County Music Adviser, and an assistant, and a great deal of practical work is done, from the advising of local societies to the organizing of a week's residential course for amateur music makers, as well as half-day schools for accompanists and conductors.

Another example of county co-ordination is provided by the Dorset Music Council, started in 1942 as a small committee to encourage amateur music-making in the county. When the need for a focal point for activities was realized, a fund was opened (the subscribers to which are called the Friends of Music in Dorset) a small hall was secured in Blandford, and equipped as a music centre. Holding about forty people, with a grand piano installed, the centre makes a pleasant meeting place for school classes, rehearsals, practices, small concerts, etc. A joint enterprise with the centre is the Dorset Rural Music School, inaugurated in 1948, which sponsors classes in the violin and other instruments at schools and in villages surrounding Blandford.

Unlike the Bournemouth Symphony Orchestra, whose roots go back to the end of the last century, the Southern Philharmonic Orchestra represents an entirely new and post-war regional development. It was formed in 1945 under the direction of Herbert Menges, musical director of the Brighton Philharmonic Society. It began as much as an act of faith as anything, for nobody knew how many regular concerts the Brighton audiences would support, nor what other engagements would have to be taken. Fortunately some financial backing was provided by the Brighton Corporation and the Arts Council, and encouraged by this the Society has quickly built up a large musical following in the south of England. To-day, the Southern Philharmonic Orchestra plays regularly not only at the Dome, Brighton, but at Southampton, Portsmouth, Eastbourne, Croydon and many other districts of Kent, Sussex, Surrey and Hampshire.

Out of his experience with this venture Herbert Menges has evolved a definite conception for organizing the regional music of Britain. He thinks that the country should be roughly divided into regions, each with its own orchestra and each free from uncontrolled competition from outside its borders. This would not mean that music lovers in one region would hear no other orchestras, for mutual exchange between regions would constantly be arranged. In that way something like real security would be available to orchestral musicians, whereas at present orchestras are simply cutting each other's throats, in Mr. Menges' opinion.

The various B.B.C. Regional Stations have, of course, helped greatly in the musical education of the British people. I describe the work of the B.B.C. in another chapter, but it is interesting here to glance at the work of one region, the Midland. This station broadcasts a great number of concerts by the City of Birmingham and other local orchestras, as well as sponsoring various musical series, like "Midland Organs and Organists" and "The Musician at the Gramophone".

The Midland Regional has also organized contests for works by Midland composers: in one of these, out of a total of 124 works submitted, twenty-five were adjudged up to standard and performed. In another series, listeners' questions on musical subjects have been answered by an expert, while the B.B.C. Midland Orchestra illustrated points raised.

The Scottish, Welsh and Northern Ireland Regions, on the other hand, have a different sort of musical fare for their public, for in those regions there exists a wealth of rich folk-music. Thus, the Northern Ireland station concentrates on a definite musical pattern in their programmes: choral music—such as the fortnightly "Sing As We Go" and hymn-singing: vocal music—recitals and ballad concerts; traditional dance-music— played by fiddlers, pipers, ceilidhe bands and folk orchestras. In order to facilitate and maintain this service, members of the Region's Music Department are continually touring the country holding auditions and attending local concerts in search for talent (the result of these researches being heard in a regular "Concert from the Country" programme).

The orchestra is only one facet of the musical world, and offers in some ways a restricted amount of opportunity for the amateur. Choirs and amateur opera companies give a wider scope, and their numbers in Britain must be

legion. There is something essentially regional
and local about choral singing. One of its delights
is that more often than not the choirs make great
use of local songs in their repertoire. Some of the
fishermen's choirs from the east coast of England,
or the Welsh and Cornish choirs, are a treat and
a joy to listen to, singing songs that are a living
part of the traditional life and singing them as
no "foreign" group could sing. It can hardly be
insignificant that choral singing excels among the
less populated areas. Unless you were to visit
the English Folk House near Regent's Park you
would be hard put to find any good folk-singing
in London—and it would be still more useless
searching around Tooting or Balham, Raynes
Park or Surbiton. But every Saturday night, and
sometimes other nights, too, you will hear the old
folk songs sung in the pubs of Cornwall and
Dorset, in Londonderry and on the Isle of Skye,
up the Rhondda Valley and over in Anglesey.

Wales, of course, is renowned as the land of
song. Music plays an important part in the
programmes of a new Welsh movement, the
Welsh Federation of Music and Arts Clubs, an
association of the numerous clubs and educational
settlements which have now sprung up all over
Wales. At one of the most successful of these, the
club at the Brynmawr Settlement, it is part of the
constitution that every year a concert of modern
Welsh music shall be given. In addition, St. David's

Day is celebrated with a *Noson Lawen* with traditional Welsh music and poetry, and there are special performances of Celtic dances and folk-songs. In this way the club ensures that its members are kept aware of the strong stream of Welsh culture which is their inheritance. This is not a blindly nationalist policy, however. At other times of the year the club presents concerts of modern music from Scotland, Ireland, Norway, England, France, Russia, Czechoslovakia, America, etc. Following each concert there is a discussion. Special meetings are also held to study instrumental music, this being the weakest side of the Welsh musical tradition (since the harp became less fashionable). All meetings are held in a very friendly atmosphere, with the typical Welsh "cup of tea" always to hand. The organizers believe that this informal approach is an excellent way of getting people to take an interest in serious art.

A scheme in the same general tradition as the Welsh Music Clubs, but on a larger scale, has been started in England—namely, Rural Music Schools. The schools were first founded in Hertfordshire, "to meet the need of persons of every age—particularly those living in country places —who want to play and sing and listen to good music". They are supported by teachers, students, professional musicians, statutory and voluntary bodies, educationists and various committees who co-operate for the good of music in their area. To-day there are schools established in Hertfordshire, Wiltshire, Bedfordshire, Suffolk, Sussex, Bucks, Devon, Huntingdonshire, Lancashire and Kent. One of the most successful, the Sussex Rural Music School, has more than 700 registered pupils, attending seventy classes, for violin, piano, chamber music, orchestral and choral groups. The school is staffed by a Director, an Organizing Secretary, three Assistant Music Organizers, an office assistant and thirty professional part-time teachers, and has large headquarters in Lewes. Under the presidency of Sir Adrian Boult, the School has become the official Music Organizer and Adviser for East and West Sussex Local Education Authorities. Apart from organizing festivals and training concerts, the School sponsors an Advisory Service, a professional String Quartet and the County of Sussex Chamber Orchestra which gives more than fifty concerts a year to schools in various parts of the county.

A new and exciting focus to music and singing in the British Isles has been given by a number of festivals. For many years, for example, the annual National Eisteddfod of Wales has been the year's great event in the life of hundreds of tiny Welsh village choirs and orchestras. Long before the final event, inter-village and county contests are held that weed out the choirs, so that there is an all-the-year-round activity that keeps Welsh singers and orchestras on their toes. Whatever its failures of quality, no praise can be too high for the National Eisteddfod for continuing to act as a living focus for its country's culture.

Since the end of the war, Wales has also been the centre for an International Eisteddfod, held annually at Llangollen. Started as an experiment, it is now confirmed as a regular summer festival, to which come the choirs not only of other regions, but of other countries. Choirs from Sweden, Norway, Denmark, Spain and Italy are among those which have competed at Llangollen. Giving his presidential address at the last Eisteddfod, Mr. Harold Tudor revealed that as a result of this international "get-together", Welsh choirs have been invited to Denmark and Spain, while many other interchanges were being arranged between various countries whose representatives had met at the International Eisteddfod. Furthermore, so impressed have visitors been with the spirit and unity of the Festival, that similar events are being organized in Spain and elsewhere in Europe. Mr. Tudor hopes that machinery will subsequently be devised whereby winning choirs at one regional Eisteddfod will be supported by local funds to visit another.

"In this way, too, Welsh choirs will be able to return the compliment paid to Wales by overseas choirs coming here; Welsh choirs will have centres abroad at which they will be welcome to compete. I expect someone will say that the whole thing is impossible, as it was once suggested that this festival was impossible. Then let us again try the impossible."

Mr. Tudor's brave words are not foolhardy. Time and again in the past it has been proved how little beginnings lead to big ends. The sort of interchange that he envisages, and which is now developing, though begun and created in relation to music, will have far-reaching effects politically and socially. And if, as has been stated, music is the one international language, what better than that a love of it should serve to open up the highway to a united world?

The one obvious thing is that if a lot of rootless, traditionless groups from Clapham Common or Kensington should try to hold an "International Eisteddfod" the result would be a joke. The cardinal feature of the Llangollen event was that here was a gathering of the *native* cultures of a number of countries and regions. That seems the healthiest way of building anything, music or worlds—with hundreds of little roots that converge, and form a solid foundation to a bigger one.

The local contribution is a main feature of a number of musical festivals that have recently developed in the regions of Britain. The Cheltenham Festival and the Bath Assembly are two excellent examples, the latter being an impressive affair that captures, as well it might in such a lovely city, much of the glorious past. It would be difficult to think of a better setting for a musical festival than Bath which, in the words of one of the critics who attended the 1949 Festival, "encupped between its hills, whispers of the civilizations that have passed since Celtic times, the Britons, Romans, early English, the Elizabethans, Georgians, and Edwardians. . . . It has absorbed them all, thus acquiring harmony: the harmony of English life." Of still greater fame is the Edinburgh Music Festival, another post-war product—an astonishing case of what can be done with the right spirit and enthusiasm. Edinburgh's example, followed on a slightly smaller scale by the first fifty cities and towns of Britain, could revitalize the local and national culture of this land.

All the same the contents of the Edinburgh Festival tend to be somewhat international, and for detailed consideration I would prefer to turn to the Aldeburgh Festival of Music and Arts. This was founded in 1948 by a group of composers and musicians, led by Benjamin Britten (himself a Suffolk man), Peter Pears and Eric Crozier, under the presidency of the Earl of Harewood. The aims and tone of the Festival were set out well enough by the Earl himself, in a foreword to the programme:

"In any community, local patriotism is a strong

factor and it need not be aggressive to be effective. The art of a town or county is as logical a local product as, for instance, the county cricket team, and as much a source of pride. If the friendly rivalries and the shades of opinion, which to the visitor may seem infinitesimal, are not integral parts of this Festival programme, the intimacy, which results from them, is. The various items of the programme 'belong' to Aldeburgh and Suffolk in the sense that Mozart did to Salzburg. They are at the same time, many of them, of world-wide fame. Through them local patriotism, with its enhanced sense of physical relationship with its surroundings and its intimate local associations, finds its point of contact with the national and international."

The origins of the Festival were further outlined by Eric Crozier. The idea really began, he recalled, when he and other members of the English Opera Group were presenting Benjamin Britten's operas in Switzerland, in a Festival. There did seem something absurd about travelling so far to win success with British operas that Manchester, Edinburgh and London would not support. It was exciting to represent British music at international festivals, but the group could not hope to repeat the experiment another year.

Britten, Pears and Crozier then conceived the idea of "making their own festival" in home surroundings. Back in Aldeburgh they held a series of meetings at which enthusiasm was great. At the beginning of January, 1948, a public meeting in the Jubilee Hall, Aldeburgh, resulted in nearly £200 being subscribed in the form of guarantees against loss. During the following weeks the sum rose till it reached £1,400. Finally, extra support was given by the Arts Council and the Festival became a reality.

"Since our very first talks in Switzerland about the idea of a Festival," continued Mr. Crozier, "it has always been our intention that this should be an annual and growing event, making Aldeburgh a temporary home for leading contemporary artists in opera, drama, ballet, chamber music and painting. Expansion will depend on the creation of a demand from Suffolk audiences, for although many visitors may attend a Festival, it is on support from local people that planning for the future must be based. Plans for several years will be determined by the buildings available—the Jubilee Hall, the Parish Church, the Baptist Chapel and the Cinema—but is it over-fanciful to look forward, through a series of annual Festivals, to Aldeburgh as the centre of the arts in East Suffolk, with its own theatre for the annual visits of its Festival artists? To judge by the enthusiasm of local support in the past I do not think it is."

At the first Festival the programme included a

performance of Benjamin Britten's *Albert Herring*; a solo pianoforte recital by Mewton-Wood; recitals by Peter Pears, Benjamin Britten and George Roth, 'cello; a recital by the Zorian String Quartet; an Aldeburgh Serenade Concert; and a choral and orchestral concert by the Aldeburgh Festival Choir, drawn from the Aldeburgh Choral Society, Ipswich Choral Society, Wickham Market Church Choir, Leiston County Grammar School Choir, Ipswich Bach Choir, Ipswich Orpheus Choir, Woodbridge Choral Society, St. Felix School Choir of Southwold, and Ipswich Co-operative Society Choir. This local choir totalling well over 100 sang, among other items, Benjamin Britten's *St. Nicholas Cantata*, written at Aldeburgh during 1947-8, and also (for the first time anywhere) *God's Grandeur*, a setting of a poem by Gerard Manley Hopkins, specially composed for the Festival by Martin Shaw, another East Anglian composer.

E. M. Forster, who was a patron of the Festival, gave an interesting analysis of the reception, writing in the programme of the 1949 Festival. He thought that in Aldeburgh, home of the poet George Crabbe, around whose *The Borough* Benjamin Britten's first opera, *Peter Grimes*, was based, there existed the natural basis for a festival. It could offer a particular tradition, a special tradition, a special atmosphere which did not exist elsewhere in these islands: nothing overwhelming, but something that was its own, something of which it could be proud. He found that he much preferred seeing a performance of *Albert Herring* in the intimate confinements of a local village hall, than "in the immensities of Covent Garden, where the problem was not so much to avoid collisions, as to get into touch". Mr. Forster went on:

"It was delightful to burst out in the intervals on to the beach, or to watch the crowd who were partly in evening dress and partly dressed anyhow, and exempt from the drilled smartness of Glyndebourne. During the first interval a man in a pub said: 'I took a ticket for this show because it is local and I felt I had to. I'd have sold it to anyone for sixpence earlier on. I wouldn't part with it now for ten pounds.'"

That must have been a general local feeling, for in 1949 the Festival was repeated on a much wider scale, with performances of three of Britten's operas, as well as numerous concerts and instrumental features, including visits by the Cambridge University Madrigal Society.

I have given some space to the Aldeburgh Festival and its musical aspect (there are also exhibitions of art, lectures, etc.) as it is symptomatic of a new trend in Britain towards reviving or creating local festivals, of which music is always a main part. Often these are held in most beautiful surroundings—Edinburgh and Bath, among the bigger ones, Beaulieu Abbey or Glyndebourne in Sussex, among the smaller ones. Then there are a number of music summer schools that are, in effect, festivals, William Glock's Summer School at Bryanston, Dorset, being an excellent example. Here, in leisurely country surroundings, a week or longer is spent by a large gathering of people sampling some of the best of old and new music. A reaction to this sort of experience was expressed by a critic in the *Mercury*, Bournemouth:

"To sum up, the 1949 Summer School was a notable success, notable not only because the distinguished teachers assembled there went their way imparting wisdom, stimulus and inspiration, but also because the many superlative perform-ances to which they and others contributed com-bined to create an occasion of unusual character; not an escapist revelling in the musical glories of the past, but a festival designed to reflect precisely the tumultous, discordant, problematic present. It left one full of doubts, full of self-questionings, but alive and exhilarated as seldom before."

Such a reaction is, it is heartening to know, becoming a common one. All over Britain more and more people are being drawn to musical festivals, to general concerts and recitals, to choirs and music clubs, in a quest for an intellectual and emotional stimulus that the canned forms of entertainment cannot provide. Music is not only a food of love, but of life. That is why so much importance attaches to the regional revival in its practise and performance, especially where attempts are being made to save and recover the traditional folk-songs and melodies that reflect the whole character of our race—and without which, lost in the vulgar blarings from Tin Pan Alley, W.C.2, we would be much the poorer as a nation.

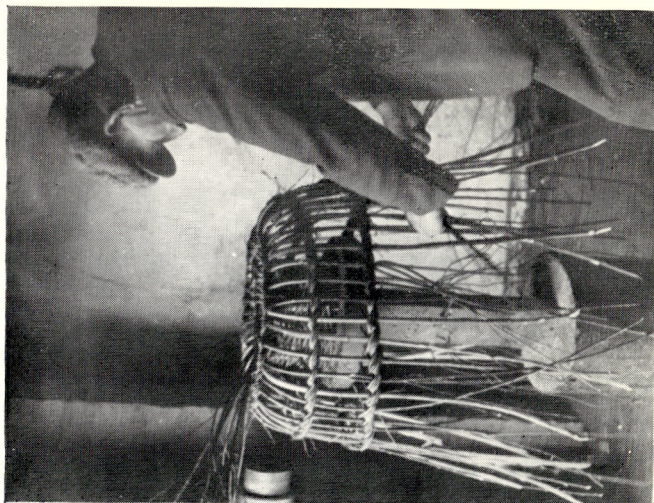

CRAB POT MAKER

WHEELWRIGHT

BERNARD LEACH AT WORK

BROADCASTING

IN less than thirty years the invention of broadcasting has become so interwoven into the pattern of our daily life that it is taken for granted. With the addition now of television, the potentialities of these new instruments for entertaining and influencing the mind of man have assumed immense proportions. Such an influence could be exerted for bad as well as good. A standardization, not so much only of ideas but also of taste, could have been imposed throughout Britain. The B.B.C. could have established a network of relay transmitters and sent out the same programme everywhere from London. But, in the words of Andrew Stewart, B.B.C. Northern Ireland Controller:

"That would not have done for the people of the United Kingdom; their individuality would have rejected the uniformity of centrally conceived, centrally performed network programmes. With them, within a large unity of purpose, diversity prevails, and indeed the unity of the whole is stronger from the different textures of the constituents. Climate, geography, occupation, and mixtures of blood, and history, have combined to produce native ways of life, attitudes to

G

God and man, habits of mind, and kinds of entertainments which are the stuff of local broadcasting and rightly have a place also in B.B.C. programmes as a whole. In each different region each Home Service makes a different selection of the native and of the general and metropolitan, each seeking to create in its programme a mixture of ideas and facts and art, which listeners will accept as their own mixture, unique as they are unique. It approaches Regional problems through the listeners' own habitual ways of thought and speech, informing listeners, with the integrity and impartiality required of the B.B.C., about the affairs and controversies which are important to them in their part of the country, broadcasting their forms of Christian worship, setting forth their character in drama, presenting their projects and activities in features, performing their music, telling their stories, reflecting their humour and projecting their entertainments and recreations."

That is the official viewpoint. Another aspect has been expressively put by Sir Thomas Beecham, describing evidence that he gave before a Royal Commission inquiring into the B.B.C. Charter.

"I concentrated my criticism upon the wholly undesirable weight of power and influence residing in the Corporation's London headquarters. I pointed out that the excessive control exercised by the centre of administration was inimical to public interest in the country by and large.

The Corporation had divided Great Britain into
so many Regional areas but had withheld from
them full freedom or independence of control or
action over their respective functions. In other
words, all of these collateral creations were being
treated as the poor relations of the bloated pluto-
crat of Portland Place. I insisted that if the
Commission perpetuated the monopoly granted
ten years previously it should do everything in
its power to mitigate its evils. It should, out of
the net sum collected by the Post Office and
passed on by it to the Corporation, allocate to
each Region a specific amount over which each
Region should have entire control. This would
enable the participants in the flow of public
money from all over the kingdom to build
up each for itself a more vigorous personal
freedom and independence. Very soon there
would develop a rivalry between them, to provide
their patrons with the best and most varied forms
of entertainment. And why not indeed? London,
like every other centre of political, legal, and
social life everywhere is too apt to indulge in the
illusion that those who live outside its hallowed
area are, in the picturesque phrase of a Minister
of the Crown, not worth a tinker's cuss. Surely
in these democratic days, when we hear and read
daily that the voice of the people is a paramount
force, it might be remembered for one brief
moment that the bulk of the inhabitants of this

distressed island do not live either in London or in its vicinity. They are condemned to drag out an uninspiring existence in those despised areas known as the provinces. It is conveniently forgotten by the worshippers at the Metropolitan shrine that the populations of Yorkshire and Lancashire exceed in number those of the whole of the south of England. And if we are to swallow the democratic dogma wholesale we should admit without argument that these many millions should have more right and opportunity to declare what it is they want to hear through the medium of broadcasting than they have at the present time. In other words, the great industrial north in particular should not be content to take its light, leading, and instruction from the arrogant south."

Sir Thomas has not been the only critic. In some parts, notably Wales and Scotland, a large number of listeners feel that programmes are not strongly regional enough. There is also the fact that even now the number of hours per week allocated to directly local matter is not very high (forty hours a week being the Scottish Regional average, for instance). On the other hand, since the resumption of regional broadcasting after the war-time hold-up, there can be no doubt that a much more enlightened policy has prevailed. The "dead hand" of Portland Place may still rest on the controls, but its touch is very light, and the consequence has been that each of the regions seems to have taken courage and ventured into new and fresher spheres.

This post-war development came just at the right time, when people wanted to resume their normal lives—wanted to emphasize, if anything, the meaning of their familiar, local life, with all its everyday idiosyncrasies and traditions. As a consequence it is interesting to note the popularity of a whole series of what are termed "audience-participation" programmes, on the regional stations. One of the first to initiate these was the Midland Regional, from Birmingham, with its "Listeners Answer Back" and "Town Forum" programmes, held at different towns and villages each week.

The procedure varies a little with each region, but the basic element of these programmes is that the B.B.C. microphone is installed in a village hall or some other large public building, and local inhabitants are invited to attend a broadcast session with their questions. Some of the most provocative of these are picked out by a question master and read out before the audience, members of which are invited to step up to the microphone and give their answers. The programmes are unrehearsed and provide a refreshing contrast to more organized programmes. Questions vary from "Are country people better fed than towns-people?" and "How much pocket-money should children have?" to questions of more specifically

local significance. (Thus, at the time when the newspapers were full of the attempts of a German professor and his daughter to sail across the Atlantic in a small open sailing boat, "Speak Your Mind" at a fishing port had a long session on whether it was fair for inexperienced people to embark on such adventurous projects and possibly risk the lives of local fishermen and life-boatmen who might have to come to their rescue.) At these broadcasts there are many spontaneous examples of local wit and humour, against a background feeling of neighbourliness.

Some of the regions have now developed these audience-participation broadcasts into a complete section of their programmes. The West Regional has "Speak Your Mind", in which local people ask and answer the questions; "Any Questions", in which a team of four, including several regular speakers like A. G. Street, Ralph Wightman and John Arlott, plus visitors of the calibre of C. E. M. Joad, Michael Foot, M.P., Michael Ayrton, answer spontaneous questions put by the audience; and "Air Space", the radio equivalent of a news-paper's correspondence column in which the B.B.C. readers read out listeners' letters expressing criticism of all manner of objects and services, from the B.B.C. to local councils. In addition, the West Regional broadcasts two special pro-grammes dealing with public affairs, "The West at Westminster", a weekly summary of Parliamentary dealings on matters in which the region is concerned, paying special attention to the activities of West-country M.P.s—and "County Commentary", a regular programme in which leading West-country journalists speak on local topics of their own choice, thus giving, in fact, a leading article over the air.

Commenting on the experience of these programmes, in a special booklet issued in 1949, the B.B.C. West Regional states:

"Taken together, this group of programmes is something quite revolutionary in our public life. It is not entirely fanciful to say that not since Wessex ceased to be a kingdom—which is going back more than somewhat—has the West had the means of forming any unified opinion about its own affairs. In this field regional broadcasting fills the gap between the national press and the local press, and should bring greater vitality to both. On many issues the West-countryman's point of view is different from the Londoner's or the Scotsman's. It is the province of regional broadcasting to reflect that distinctiveness and make it articulate—a fact that Parliament recognized when it called for the establishment of a Regional Advisory Council to ensure a 'close touch with movements of thought and opinion' in the region."

The same booklet gives a clear picture of the fundamental essentials of regional broadcasting, and how this task is tackled. First there is the gathering of daily West-country news reports from 130 special correspondents, for a regular fifteen-minutes' "News from the West Country" which follows the Home Service News. A feature of this programme are interviews recorded during the day in mobile recording cars—so that listeners can hear the voice of a statesman at a banquet in Southampton, the bustle and excitement of Bampton Pony Fair, the conversation of a Wiltshire shepherd, the roar of a new engine on test in a Bristol aircraft factory, the street scene at Helston Furry Dance—sounds which give a real feeling of being present.

Next there are the audience-participation broadcasts, which equally emphasize the local and regional aspect of the programmes. And along with them go a large number of programmes devoted to the interpretation of West-country culture—culture interpreted in its widest sense, meaning not only the arts, but the general way of life. The West Country has its own character and background. Its countryside and buildings are, for instance, quite different from those of the Fen country or the Scottish Highlands. It is not industrialized like the Midlands or the north of England. It has a very long coastline, in relation to its land area. The West-countryman is more interested in gale warnings than the Midlander, better acquainted with rural life than the Londoner, not so factory-minded as the Lancashire-man. A talk on mustard-growing would be valuable to Norfolk farmers, but useless to Cornish farmers—and so on.

These facts must all be taken into account by the programme planners, so the West Regional broadcasts special talks to western farmers and growers, religious broadcasts come not from London but from churches and chapels scattered all over the west. To meet the needs of fishermen in Devon, Cornwall and the Channel Islands, day-time gale warnings are broadcast before the one o'clock news. The interests of naturalists are catered for in no fewer than four series, all of which have been so successful that they are now broadcast nationally—"The Naturalist", "Country Questions", "Bird Song of the Month" and a monthly nature magazine, "Out of Doors".

In the sphere of the arts local talent has steadily been fostered, so that to-day when there is a broadcast of a Devonshire play by Eden Philpotts, or one of the dramatized Cornish tales of Charles Lee, actors and actresses can be cast who really can speak the local dialect. The B.B.C. policy on this point has been stated as follows:

"Regional broadcasting has the obligation to foster local talent for two reasons: because the opportunities it offers can resist the draining into London of provincial talent (and the consequent impoverishment of local life), and because each region is best fitted to provide its own distinctive style of performance. The resources of the professional stage in London cannot provide authentic casting for plays in the many regional dialects which lend diversity and richness to our language throughout the United Kingdom.

"Again, it is not enough to have thousands of music lovers dependent on the occasional visits of London orchestras, and the enterprise of the Bournemouth Municipality in forming a first-rate resident orchestra is a fine example of the sort of activity the B.B.C. West Region should—and does—support. The primacy of London as the focus of our national culture is indisputable and right; but it has been becoming too strong a magnet. One of the proudest objectives of regional broadcasting is to restore vigour and abundance and exacting standard to local forms of culture. The formation and training of the West Country Studio Orchestra and the West Country Singers are two achievements which show what can be done."

What has been done in the West Region has been repeated in other regions, but in each case on an entirely local basis. That is to say, where the essentially agricultural West Region gives emphasis to country programmes, the programmes of a more industrialized area like the north reflect a stronger leaning towards essentially north-country interests—for instance, music-hall programmes, Rugby League matches, brass band concerts. The Midland Region has presented programmes on "Midland Roads and Rivers", "Musical Counties", and "Archaeology as an Adventure"—the latter featuring six talks illustrated by descriptions of Midland sites and discoveries, such as the British Camp in the Malvern Hills, Offa's Dyke in Shropshire and the Mosaic Floor uncovered at Chedworth. From Northern Ireland is broadcast a regular "Village Picture", a broadcaster going to a remote Ulster village and talking to local inhabitants until he has obtained enough information, some of it recorded direct, to give a fascinating glimpse of the life there. In these programmes the extreme individuality and variety of speech comes out well; a metallic clipped speech from one area, a slow, rhythmical speech from another; here an Elizabethan phrase, there a Scottish or Gaelic word. This individuality even within a small region, lends an added attraction to such Northern Ireland features as the reading of short stories, or of poetry, and of course to drama (about forty plays a year are broadcast).

One of the most active of the B.B.C. Regions is the Northern, whose programmes serve more than one-third of the total area of England. It was from here that Wilfred Pickles's famous "Have a Go" programmes originated, and among many other typically northern features are, or have been, "Blackpool Nights", "Northern Music Hall",

"Liverpool—Portrait of a City", "A Great Ship Sails", "Farmer Bewick's Barn Dances", "Down the Tyne", "The Arts in the North" and "Know your Region". Phyllis Bentley, well-known novelist, has written of the teeming abundance of material, an inexhaustible stock of character and story, which the north of England offers to the creative artist.

"Partly this is due to the great variety of our geography. Because of the varied physical contours and contents of our land, in the north we have many different occupations. We are fishermen, farmers, shepherds, miners and makers of textiles, ships and steel. So that though our basic character is much the same, our ways of life and the effect events have upon us are very various. Now the great source of art, as of pleasure, is variety. Variety means contrast, and contrast means the possibility of conflict, and all stories are founded upon conflict.

"Another great stock of northern material which northern writers may turn into art is our abundant local history and legend. This is recorded in old letters and diaries, in the researches of historians, and in tradition, handed down by word of mouth. The northern novelist and dramatist can steep himself in these abundant old records and in contemporary northern life, and then use the past to interpret the significance of the present.

"It is not to be wondered at then, that the North Region is rich in writers and artists of every kind. But I wish it could be richer still. I should like to see a great blossoming, a great burgeoning forth, of art of all kinds in the north. Then our great region would be fully and magnificently expressed, its character and qualities would become widely known and its contribution to European life would be realized and appreciated. The great part which the B.B.C. can and does play in stimulating the art of our region is clearly visible in its varied programmes."

It was the Northern Region that made history with the first broadcast in Britain from a City Council meeting (from Kingston-upon-Hull). Old traditions and crafts are dealt with in such broadcasts as those of cheese-making in Wensleydale, of the thousand-year-old nightly "Wakeman" ceremony from Ripon, of the unloading of the fishing fleets at Fleetwood. The Region's "Children's Hour" lays great stress on local activities, through such programmes as "Know Your Region", "Nomad's Walks", and a series of children's concerts featuring northern songs and music. Yorkshire dialect stories are another regular feature, together with other programmes stressing the use of local dialect, "Angler's Arms" and "Northern Scene".

In Scotland, feature programmes form an important part of the Region's broadcasting programmes. Among typical items have been a dramatized history of the war service of the famous river steamers of the Clyde Pleasure Fleet; a professional portrait of a Scottish Merchant Navy Radio Officer; a portrait of a Glasgow Stage Manager who has been the backroom boy of everything from pantomime to Shakespeare, circuses to Sarah Bernhardt; a programme on the running of a big Scottish railway terminus; and the history of a Scottish town celebrating its Diamond Jubilee. "Theatre in Scotland", a fortnightly series of broadcasts by the main Scottish Repertory Companies, interwoven with talks and discussions, has done a lot to revive interest in local theatres. "Chapbook" presents an interview with a leading Scottish author or musician, and "Arts Review" gives a regular broadcast criticism of contemporary Scottish art. In the musical sphere the Region endeavours to broadcast at least one work by a Scottish composer every month, while there is a wealth of pro-grammes devoted to Scottish folk-songs, pipe music, ceilidhes, etc.

Most purely regional of all the Scottish broad-cast programmes, are those arranged by the Gaelic Section, and broadcast in Gaelic. The organizers have found that there is an unspoiled naturalness about the Highlander that makes him an excellent broadcaster, while the simple culture of the Highlands lends itself easily to radio.

Naturally, if unfortunately, the amount of broadcasting in the Gaelic language is limited, but it is rightly considered as vital that the service should be provided so long as there is a section of Gaelic-speaking people. Melville Dinwiddie, Controller of Programmes, Scottish Region, has stated:

"But the decline of the Gaelic language and the burden of distance make the task of broadcasting it difficult both in war and peace. Programmes in Gaelic have been broadcast for nearly twenty years. It has been argued that the maintenance, indeed the survival of the Gaelic language, is bound up with the policy of the B.B.C. True, whatever is included or omitted from the Scottish programmes will have its effect upon the future of this ancient and expressive language. But the aim of the Gaelic Section of the B.B.C. must be to exploit to the full the entertainment and cultural wealth of its song and story, and the pipe and fiddle tunes which are so woven into the life of the Highlands. Many of those who can best reflect Gaelic culture are to be found only in the glens and islands of the north. Our recording cars have gone from Campbeltown to the Butt of Lewis, from Kingussie to Barra in search of talent. The result has been programmes with a rich mixture of the old and the new, the traditional action songs and the bardic story, the Ceilidhe and the modern con-

cert. Close co-operation with An Comunn Gaid-
healach has resulted in many broadcasts from the
Annual Mod. The Crowning of the Bard, the
actual competitions, and the prize-winning choirs
and soloists, together with an impression of the
enthusiasm and healthy rivalry of these meetings,
command a very large audience, and reveal the
keenness of both Gaelic and non-Gaelic speaking
listeners for this remarkable gathering. Time will
show whether any definite influence on standards
of performance is made, but the hearing in
clachans and island villages of the attempts of
others should result in a general improvement and
greater desire to compete and win. Broadcasting
has also provided a valuable service to Gaelic
listeners in isolated places by News Bulletins,
discussions on the peculiar problems of the
Highlands, and information about current affairs.
Care is required to preserve a balance of dialect.
Radio has done more than any other agency to
find a common denominator of Gaelic speech,
and to maintain the purity of a language which
lives on as a cultural influence."

In Wales there is also a double-language
system of broadcasts, with the exception that
considerably more time is allowed for Welsh-
speaking programmes than for the Gaelic in
Scotland. There would, indeed, be an uproar in
the Principality if Welsh-speaking programmes
were diminished, for there are, after all, nearly

1,000,000 Welsh-speaking inhabitants. For this reason, and especially as so many of these people are to the forefront in the social and intellectual life of Wales, a great deal of pressure is constantly brought to bear on the Welsh Region planners. Wales is possibly, at least in the sense of language, the most independent of all the regional stations (though for initiative in developing local cultural trends I would share the prize with the West Region). Even where they are broadcast in English, the Welsh Region's programmes have an unmistakably Celtic flavour of their own, as could be noticed in that lively variety programme, "Welsh Rarebit", before it was put on the Light Programme and devitalized to suit English audiences.

Unlike many of the other regions, Wales is fortunate in being able to broadcast a number of events that are bound up in the ancient traditions of the land, and still as vital as ever. Notable among these is the National Eisteddfod, which is held every year alternatively in a North and South Wales town. For a whole week, the Welsh Regional Programme is very largely devoted to this great national festival—an excellent example of how broadcasting can help to strengthen the development of national tradition. Other Welsh events, such as choir contests, are also featured regularly on the Welsh Region, which is fortunate, too, in being able to draw on a wide range of

H

Welsh dramatists, poets and story-tellers—among them Emlyn Williams, Jack Jones, Richard Hughes, Rhys Davies, Gwyn Jones, Dylan Thomas, Cliff Gordon. If one were to compare the literary quality and standard of the average Welsh programme with those of other regions, the comparison would almost certainly be in favour of Wales. This is as it should be, for there has recently been a Welsh Renaissance in literature, and no other region could produce an equal list of gifted and imaginative writers. At the same time, part of this development is due to enterprise on the part of Welsh producers, who are not afraid to put on experimental programmes, or to commission writers to do some imaginative piece of reporting. Sometimes the experiments may fail, but they are no less the worth trying.

Indeed, the scope for experimenting in regional broadcasting remains abundant. Recently, for instance, on the North Regional, James R. Gregson, then Drama Director, hit on the idea of "Three-Decker" adaptations of full-scale northern novels. Instead of following the usual practice of cutting the novels up into thirteen half-hour readings, chapter by chapter, Gregson took the novels to pieces and rebuilt them as radio plays of three acts or parts. In this way such books as Winifred Holtby's *South Riding*, Emily Brontë's *Wuthering Heights*, Priestley's *Good Companions* and Howard Spring's *Fame is the Spur* were presented with a new freshness of touch. In Scotland, the Schools Section hit on an original way of presenting home geography as an exciting subject by putting on a series "Exploring Scotland", built up around the adventures of a man and a boy searching for another man. This other man knows he is being looked for and keeps on the run, trying to conceal himself in many parts of Scotland and adopting many occupations—in a factory, a farm, the fishing fleet and so on. The search takes the man and boy into almost every corner of Scotland and brings them into touch with widely differing occupations and social conditions.

Such programmes as "Schools" and talks, particularly the latter, represent perhaps the most direct educational influences of the B.B.C. regions, and one cannot help wishing that their scope was more extensive. On the West Regional for instance, during the course of a typical week, the number of specific West-country talks will seldom exceed half-a-dozen, compared with at least twice as many talks of national interest broadcast in the Service from London. The talks of local interest that are given are often of such educative and entertainment value—reminiscences of famous West-country historical figures, studies of writers, reconstructions of memorable events—that the appetite is whetted and left unsatisfied. Probably much the same impression is left in other regions. There is a case here for the Regional Planner to gather together a team of first-class regional writers for broadcasting, and in the second place to send them out to seek the old and new stories of local initiative and drama which have been the making of the region. It is not long since the regional paper, *Wales*, commented "It would do most of the Anglo-Welsh poets no harm to rough it, walk through the whole land and see what it is like." The same might be said of any region, and it might well be possible for the B.B.C. to give a lead encouraging a crusade of this or some similar nature.

I have given a brief picture of the activities of the various B.B.C. Regional Stations, though not of the Home Service from London. There is no reason why the latter should not be as much a regional programme as any other, but in fact it lacks to a very large extent all the "local" qualities that lend such an air of originality to the regional programmes. On the Home Service the programmes are of a high intellectual and entertainment standard (and quite often include some of the best of the regional items, re-broadcast). But there is no sense of an entity, of a whole, nor even of any of that real character which, however uncertainly, can be traced on the regional programmes. That there is a place, and a vital one, for a national programme making available the cream of all regional broadcasting, no one could deny. At the same time, it seems a great pity that the peoples of London and the Home Counties of England are not served by their own Regional Station, which might gradually do much to revive all those dwindling customs, traditions, arts and crafts and ways of life that once shaped the face of that particular area. Essex, Kent, Sussex, Surrey, Bucks and Berks—London itself—must all be rich with material and still, to some extent, with local characters. Yet they have no audience-participation programmes. A pity that the B.B.C. microphone does not regularly go out among the fields and lanes of some of these Home Counties, a pity that there are no programmes from a Wapping inn or a Chiltern pub, such as have been done by the Midland Region from Cotswold public houses.

Such an idea, the development of a Home Counties Regional Programme, may seem superfluous at first—but the more it is considered the more significant it will appear. It is the whole curse and cause of our present devitalized state that Britain as a nation has become centralized and standardized to an extent undreamed of by even the most daring planners of the past. Ironically enough, it is the planners themselves who are now awakening to the dangers of this trend, hence the furore of town and country planning, regional boards and so on. The B.B.C. is one such planner. At one time there were strong factions in the Corporation that favoured closing down regional programmes as such. To-day the view has swung round. It is realized that the B.B.C. has the task, indeed the duty, of encouraging the revival of regionalism. In this endeavour it is one of many bodies, originally national in conception, which are becoming more and more decentralized. The reward for these efforts is being found in a much warmer and closer contact with the listening public. This is demonstrated when, as sometimes happens, a B.B.C. Region sends out a team of its leading officials as a Brains Trust to some village or town hall, to answer the public's questions. Such gatherings are packed out, some extremely pertinent and intelligent questions are asked and answered, and another link is forged between sponsors and recipients of a public service. How one wishes officials of some of the remote Government departments would follow suit!

And so, if the trend is to be followed out logically, perhaps the day will come when the B.B.C. does open a Home Counties Station. When, indeed, the development of regional broadcasting goes much further, so that even within a region there are sub-stations. The basis of this exists already in Scotland, where there is a separate Aberdeen Station, and in Wales, where there is the Bangor Station. In the West Country, too, there are studios not only at Bristol, but at Plymouth, Exeter, Bournemouth and Redruth.

In the B.B.C. we see reflected through the pattern of one organization the public trend away from centralization. For, make no mistake, the increased attention given to regional requirements has not come philanthropically from the B.B.C. alone. Public opinion has exerted an influence that is not always realized. If the public's desires to emphasize its essentially local life were to slacken, then in the nature of things this would be reflected in an equal slackening off of the regional facilities provided and encouraged not only by the B.B.C. but by other bodies like the Arts Council. Fortunately, so far, the tendency has been quite the other way. There is every hope, such is the influence of the spoken word, that all over Britain broadcasting is helping to establish a permanent regional consciousness which will not easily be weakened again.

EDUCATION

EDUCATION, like entertainment or industrial development, has always been national in policy, regional in practice. This is not by any means a healthy state of affairs, for it may result in a policy being forced upon some areas where local conditions render such a policy quite unsuitable. Or a national policy may be used as a political weapon, which is what happened in Wales when the compulsory teaching of English and the virtual side-tracking of the teaching of Welsh inevitably weakened the Welsh sense of nationhood.

To-day, more than ever before, the education of British youth is directed from a single headquarters, the Ministry of Education. The Education Act of 1944, reducing the number of Local Education Authorities from 315 to 146, strengthened the centralization of the conduct of education. Contributing to this trend has been the inevitable reduction and weakening of the country's private and "public" schools. It is possible to look ahead (not a long way) and see the final educational framework, a nation-wide system of state schools and colleges, using standard educational methods.

That is the broad picture, and it may seem a somewhat unpromising one from a regional point of view. It becomes more encouraging if we attend less to the fountainhead, and instead go out and about and study education in the regions in practice. Then developments can be seen in perspective, and it can be realized that no matter what national directives may be issued, in the long run they are conditioned by the individualizing influences of local customs and ways of life. The proof of this can be seen, again, in the case of Wales where the imposition of English standards, although immediately harmful, resulted ultimately in a wave of Welsh nationalism—which, in its turn, encouraged the re-study of the Welsh language, the development of many dormant Welsh activities, the great strengthening and widening of the Welsh Eisteddfod and other Welsh events, and so on.

Fortunately, the Ministry of Education is one of the more enlightened of Government departments. In recent years it has shown an awareness of the importance of regionalism by granting a good deal of local freedom, within the general framework of the national educational system. Thus, in 1947, the Ministry set up Regional Priority Officers, with headquarters in Newcastle, Leeds, Manchester, Leicester, Birmingham, London, Reading, Bristol and Cardiff, Cambridge and Tunbridge Wells. The duties of these Regional Officers has been to make an effective link between the Local Education Authorities and regional representatives of various Government Departments, such as the Ministry of Works. Although they only took office in 1947 these Regional Officers have done much to speed up the building and expansion of schools.

In another sphere, the training of teachers, the Ministry has also encouraged development on a regional rather than a centralized basis. Britain has been divided into a series of areas, each of which has a special educational centre which aims, in the words of the McNair Committee, "to serve as a focus of interest and activity, not only for students in training and the staffs responsible for them, but also for practising teachers in all types of institutions in the area, and for the authorities themselves". These centres are organized through the co-operation of universities, training colleges and local education authorities, in association with the Ministry of Education. Teachers receive the main part of their training there, and are also "apprenticed out to various schools in the area, to get actual working experience. By gaining their experience of teaching in the area where they will actually practice, teachers are thus more likely to be able to deal with the inevitable local problems involved in their work."

Schools, primary, secondary and grammar, in

whatever part of Britain they may be—are gradually beginning to reflect the benefits of the increased care and attention now being given to education. There are difficulties—shortage of teachers, of building materials, etc.—but against these, great strides have been made on the health and welfare side. Thanks to financial grants (generally not less than 90 per cent. of the approved expenditure) most country and provincial schools as well as city schools now provide lunches for their pupils, as well as much more efficient medical care. This benefits not only the children, but also the parents, who are granted rather more leisure and freedom than in the past. Academically, many improvements have been introduced, the effect of which is to make it much easier for children, no matter where they live, to pass, via scholarships, to grammar schools, colleges and universities. Curricula, too, have become more in tune with the times. Boys and girls who show no real aptitude for dead languages have much better facilities for learning trades which might be more useful to them in adult life. At the same time consideration is given to the less common case of students whose leaning is towards art, or crafts. (Indeed, the whole educational attitude to art in schools has become greatly improved, and to-day every town and even village school takes a pride in students' artistic efforts, which are often the subject of special local exhibitions. Various national contests are held to which boys and girls from schools all over Britain send in pictures and drawings. The quality of these have so frequently drawn praise from critics that I need hardly stress the value of this trend.)

All these developments, along with the raising of the school-leaving age to fifteen, represent a healthy expansion of the British educational system. Perhaps more interesting still, for its importance as a regional activity, has been the development of what is known as Further Education. It was probably the war years, with all their deprivations, that kindled to a flame the widespread yearning among young men and women—and not so young men and women—for some way of carrying on and intensifying the education which they began at school. Until recently, the opportunities for adult education in Britain were woefully limited, despite the good work done in the past by many pioneer technical colleges. By and large it was true to say that anyone who wanted to receive Further Education would have to put himself out considerably to obtain it. Quite likely he would have to travel some distance to receive it, and equally likely he would be involved in some extra expense. What has been needed has been a readily available *local* service of Further Education.

To-day, slowly, such a position is being

achieved. The development was encouraged by the report of the Percy Committee on Higher Technological Education, one of whose main recommendations was that a series of Regional Advisory Councils should be established and that as an integral part of the regional machinery Regional Councils should create Regional Academic Boards of Technology, composed of heads of universities and technical colleges and members of their teaching staffs. Commenting upon this report, the Ministry of Education stated:

"It has now become an accepted principle that the organization of Further Education must be upon a regional basis if all the needs of industrial and commercial personnel are to be covered adequately. It is generally recognized that on the grounds of economy alone it would be improper, particularly in the higher range of studies, for each Authority to attempt to provide for all the needs of students living in their area. Already, therefore, in most regions of the country, local education authorities have agreed to some measure of co-operation in the provision of advanced courses in technology and commerce.

"But economy is only one factor in regional organization . . . there are many positive functions which a regional body can usefully perform. These include such matters as the maintenance of contact with industry; the review of courses and curricula; advice on financial arrangements for dealing with "out-county" students; arranging for the most effective use of specialist staff and other matters."

The new Regional Councils that have been set up cover wide areas, and in many cases have been further sub-divided. The Ministry has planned ten such councils, comprising Metropolitan and Home Counties, Southern, Western, West Midlands, East Midlands, East Anglia, Yorkshire, North Western, Northern, and Wales and Monmouthshire. The Ministry's policy is that each council should be free to develop along its own lines but that it should (1) include among its members representatives of local education authorities, universities, technical colleges, industry and commerce; (2) operate its work through a number of executive or sub-committees; (3) set up an industrial advisory committee. It is interesting to note that at the time these councils were being set up in 1946, the Ministry of Education stressed that it agreed with the Percy Committee that all schemes of regional organization need not follow one and the same pattern in all particulars.

The Ministry have also set up Regional Boards for Advanced Technology whose function is "to advise the governing bodies of the participating institutions and the Regional Advisory Councils on the development and the co-ordination of higher technological studies in each institution and in the region as a whole". Membership of each board is about twenty-five. In 1948 a National Advisory Council on Education for Industry and Commerce was set up to co-ordinate the work of the Regional Councils and Academic Boards.

Such is the administrative background of Further Education, which to-day has been developed to a high degree through technical colleges, training colleges, universities and adult educational centres. It has been an important part of the Government policy for the official departments to remain in the background as much as possible. The Ministry of Education provides grants, and where necessary supervision, but otherwise responsibility and initiative is left to local organizations. This, too, has resulted in the encouragement of local initiative, and it would be possible to give innumerable fascinating accounts of Further Education in practice. Let us, here, take one very good typical example, that of the Pendley Residential Centre of Informal Education, at Tring, Hertfordshire.

Pendley was started at the end of the war. Its founder, Dorian Williams, was fortunate in having available the use of an old manor house, containing sixty rooms, solidly built and set in 100 acres of fine parkland on the edge of the lovely Chiltern Hills. Nowhere could there be a better example of the advantage of escaping from the whirl and rattle of city life, and undoubtedly a large part of Pendley's success has been due to the fact that it has its roots deep in the background and history of one of Britain's oldest regions. During the first four years of its operation more than 9,000 people attended some 250 courses, the latter being held mostly at week-ends and in mid-week, but some spreading over durations of one and even two weeks. In addition there have been more than 30,000 attendances at the various cultural activities arranged especially for non-residents.

The activities of Pendley are divided into several sections. In the first place, there are a series of week-end courses designed to appeal to all classes, having as their subjects a series of themes—"The Arts", "The English Countryside", "Music and the Amateur", "Drama and the Amateur", "Self-expression in Speech and Writing". In general these are spread over four week-ends, each about six weeks apart, with each week-end's proceedings complete in themselves. There are lectures and recitals, and special attention is paid to the participation of pupils wherever that is possible (i.e. in the course on drama a play is read and acted).

Then there are Mid-week Courses, from Tuesdays to Fridays, which are designed to introduce new leisure interests to ordinary men and women. One popular series has the title "This England",

and aims at stimulating an interest in the social history of Britain, its music, art and literature, its science and its current problems. To these mid-week courses, by arrangement with various industrial firms and local authorities groups of workers are sent from surrounding centres (i.e. workers from Vauxhall Motors, at Luton). These courses are known as non-vocational: there are also mid-week vocational or semi-vocational courses, such as one held periodically for Police Officers. At these, each morning starts with a talk to widen appreciation of professional problems and to give information about recent developments in the field of police work, the talk to be followed by group discussions and a report back. Later sessions, however, are devoted to matters of more general educational value, such as social history, the arts, science and current affairs.

Yet another feature of Pendley's system are special six-day industrial courses for foremen and supervisors, organized in co-operation with the British Institute of Management. Some of the subject titles are: "The Foreman's Place in the Management Structure", "Problems of Human Relations", "Planning for Production", and "The Foreman and the Specialist Departments". One of the great values of these courses lies in the opportunity given for meeting colleagues from other firms in a place far removed from

I

their everyday environment. During 1949 some 350 foremen and supervisors, having an aggregate responsibility for about 30,000 workers and coming from no fewer than 350 firms, each spent four days at Pendley.

When Pendley was opened principally as a residential centre it was decided to run non-resident activities as well, in order that the centre could become thoroughly associated with the neighbourhood. In the beginning there were talks on current affairs, an art class, musical appreciation, play reading, plastics. The Music Appreciation class developed into a Pendley Choir; the students studying plastics turned to pottery, and now Pendley has its own Pottery, operating with the use of clay that has been found in the manor grounds; and the play reading turned into a Drama Group of such dimensions that it enters several teams at local drama festivals. To-day the Art Group is stronger than ever, with periodical exhibitions of its work, and there are numerous new groups—Country Dancing, for example.

Describing the development, Dorian Williams emphasized that the various classes became a group, as opposed to a class, and that their existence depends on two things—their association with Pendley and their ability to do something for Pendley as well as learn something *from* Pendley.

"The success of these groups is due to many

things. Firstly, they are fulfilling a need for active as opposed to passive participation in an art; secondly, they are giving what one might term social refreshment and contact in addition to instruction; thirdly, they are bound by a loyalty not to a single teacher of a pet subject but to the parent centre.

"The value of all this was emphasized when the Drama Group, anxious to do something a little more ambitious for its annual Open Air Production, suggested that all the groups should combine in a production of Shakespeare's *Henry VIII*. So it was that with a cast finally numbering eighty-six, there were six songs from the Choir, sets of dances by two teams of Pendley Country Dancers, decor by the art group, goblets and decorations by the Pottery; even the costumes were made by the Pendley Women's Afternoon Group.

"This corporate effect was a huge success, not only because it ultimately drew audiences of nearly 4,000 with a profit to the centre of £250, but also because it gave a unity to the various groups working within Pendley. Except as a part of a centre this would not have been possible. Each group, though complete in itself, is gaining from the realization that their particular favourite art is of even greater value to them when it becomes part of a whole. It is the opportunity, and indeed the duty, of a centre—residential or nonresidential—to be the roof supported not mush-room-like and lop-sided on a single stick—but four-square and solid on finely balanced pillars, which in return get the shelter and the co-ordina-tion of purpose that the roof can give."

I have outlined in some detail the activities of Pendley, for it is representative in general of a whole band of such centres that have developed in Britain. Many of them not only cater for local and visiting people, but also entertain students from abroad (at Pendley, during 1949, there were girl students from Switzerland, Austria, France, Holland and Denmark). In this way the international aspect is stressed alongside the local and national. Indeed, in many of these centres it would seem that the perfection of a social order is found—the roots local, the activities general, the attendance international. It is therefore encouraging to learn that recently some nineteen such centres banded together into an Association calling itself the Conference of Wardens of Short Term Colleges. The aim of these might well be summed up in the words of the Minister of Edu-cation who said that "in providing for ordinary men and women opportunities for 'leisure to grow wise', adult educational centres are con-tributing something of genuine value to the stream-lined times that must inevitably be asso-ciated with the twentieth century".

The residential type of centre is by no means

the only form of Further Education. There are a number of organizations which hold classes in a particular area, or over a number of areas. Outstanding among these is the Workers' Education Association which, though it covers the whole of Britain, is essentially regional in its approach and organization. It is very seldom that the W.E.A. will agree to hold a class unless a sufficient number of people first form a group that will undertake the responsibility of guaranteeing a minimum attendance. Not only is this good economics, but it acts as an added incentive upon people to give a more active support than might otherwise be the case.

All over the country the W.E.A. has its own full-time organizers, each responsible for a given area. These organizers plan out lectures and discussions, as well as regular classes on a variety of subjects, history, mathematics, current affairs, book binding, pottery, art appreciation, etc. In some cases the organizers themselves might take a class, but in general once a definite group audience has been arranged, a lecturer is provided either from within the area, or from further afield. Courses of lectures usually total twelve per session, at the rate of one a week. They are held in the evenings, in a small hall or library room, or sometimes a private house. The lecturers are experts in their subjects, very often men and women of some eminence. For the payment of a few shillings, perhaps a pound for a session, a group of local people are given a new understanding of the world which must inevitably broaden their everyday life.

Another feature of W.E.A. activities is the holding of special week-end conferences and "colleges", attended by people from many of the weekly classes. For these conferences the Association hires a guest house or large private house, or perhaps a small school, and visitors have an opportunity to mix together in a friendly and informal atmosphere. There are lectures, discussions, recitals and socials. Those who attend these W.E.A. week-ends return to their own localities refreshed and stimulated, and what they have to say about their experiences inevitably helps to widen interest in W.E.A. activities. Recently, too, the W.E.A. has been organizing film performances. In many of the smaller towns of regional Britain now, as well as in some of the more enterprising villages, you may discover a poster announcing a series of W.E.A. films. In the main these consist of classic silent films of the past, which form a most educational background to a better understanding of the film to-day.

In this book there is not space to discuss fully the British university system, but it is most relevant to note that as a whole our universities and university colleges are organized regionally. Cambridge, London, Reading, Oxford, Southampton, Exeter, Bristol, Cardiff, Aberystwyth, Bangor, Liverpool, Manchester, Leeds, Sheffield, Nottingham, Newcastle, Edinburgh, Glasgow, Belfast—it is possible to trace out a map which would show a most healthy distribution of these centres of learning. There is certainly no London domination in the university world, and little likelihood of the familiar bugbear of centralization arising. In the past, unfortunately, universities have suffered from that other bugbear of class distinction, a sort of financial closed shop. To-day, and for the future, the trend is towards a breaking down of these barriers. Universities, and with them the complementary adult education centres and colleges, would certainly seem to offer a comprehensive choice of educational facilities to the young people of Britain, no matter where they live. If examined more closely it might be found that some of the more isolated parts are a little hardly served—there is, for instance, no university up in Cumberland and the Lake District region (Carlisle would seem a good centre). But it is a measure of the optimism that exists for the future that one takes it for granted that such omissions will soon be remedied.

Education is a broad subject. Many would suggest it is life itself. Schools and universities are simply the framework of the administrative organization through which we receive our initial education, of the textbook and blackboard variety.

Even while we are there attending these establishments, our worldly education is progressing every day. As we grow older and develop our perceptions, we learn to shape and direct this greater education. So we follow out interests in industry, or in travel, in nature study, music, literature, drama, painting, and many similar subjects which are dealt with later in this book. In the course of these experiences we widen our horizons by gaining an insight into the great art and developments of other countries and other people. This is all to the good, provided it is measured against established background. The most beautiful painting of a Chinese bird can never have quite the same reality to us as our own actual observation of a bird perched in a tree branch, on the way to work. It is the same with education. What we learn out of books about French history and German economics must always be balanced against what we learn from the life around us. It is one of the merits of the modern educational trend that this balance is being steadily adjusted. Classes are becoming more alive, aligned with the day's reality; nature studies move out of the classroom into the woods, art students set up their easels in the village High Street, readers on politics hold mock elections, domestic science trainees go and work in hotels. In many schools, classes are commissioned to carry out studies of local government, perhaps actually helping the local council by conducting housing surveys or assisting in local libraries. Boys and girls, students of all ages, share all these experiences as groups, as local units. With the best will in the world it would be difficult to educate a child one week in London, the next in Manchester, the next in Paris, and so on. It might be done, perhaps has been done, but with questionable results. Education needs the background of the familiar against which to fully experience the unfamiliar, roots with which to oppose ideas of rootlessness.

That is why, of all our activities, education is essentially one of the most regional in conception. Not so much because the law orders that it should be, but because in fact our way of life makes it impossible for it not to be so. We are born and grow up in an environment of one sort or another, but an environment that is within the bounds of our comprehension—a village, a town, a group of familiar places and people. Out of this we draw much of our strength and character, and it is my contention that it becomes our duty, as well as our natural tendency, to give back what we gain as we develop into the maturity of adult life. The educational developments that I have outlined show, I hope, that facilities are being increasingly provided which encourage the regional renaissance.

INDUSTRY

THE folly of centralization has been demonstrated in no uncertain way by the industrial development of Britain in the past hundred and fifty years. Industrialists and builders seemed to follow one another like sheep, setting up hundreds of factories and thousands of houses—all within the same crowded areas. This sort of policy was responsible for the great congestion in towns which possessed advantages for industrial enterprise (i.e. those situated on or near coalfields, or in vicinity of large ports). When the congested conditions became intolerable, the "monstrous suburban sprawl" began, resulting in the loss of much productive agricultural land (according to the Report of the Committee of Land Utilization in Rural Areas, between 1927-39, an annual average of 60,000 acres was taken over for building and constructional work). The setting up of new industries on undeveloped land in the vicinity of already flourishing industrial centres also had a deleterious effect on agricultural production. The noxious fumes and poisonous effluents discharged by certain types of factories ruined crops and made streams and rivers running through neighbouring farms unfit for watering cattle.

These trends can be traced in each of the seven main areas of Britain where industry has been concentrated—namely, London and the Home Counties; Lancashire; West Riding; Nottinghamshire and Derbyshire; Staffordshire, Warwickshire, Worcestershire, Leicestershire and Northamptonshire; Northumberland and Durham; Mid-Scotland; and Glamorgan and Monmouthshire. Basic industries like mining, shipbuilding, iron and steel manufacture and textiles, were established near their motive power and source of supply. The development was perpetuated because flourishing industries not only create conditions favourable to their own expansion but also stimulate the establishment of subsidiary industries. And so, by 1937, according to the Ministry of Town and Country Planning, no less than 79 per cent. of the insured population of Britain were resident in London, Birmingham, Manchester, Merseyside, Tyneside, West Yorkshire and Glasgow. (26 per cent. lived in London and the Home Counties alone—out of the net increase of 644 factories in Britain between 1932 and 1937, no less than 532 were located in London).

In a survey of the position issued by the Royal Commission on the Distribution of the Industrial Population, it was commented that "too often these great conurbations are characterized by (*a*) inner areas of narrow streets where houses, factories and other industrial establishments are intermixed without plans, where building has proceeded without regard to the need for preserving open spaces, and where the ill-effects of smoke and noise are very considerable indeed, and (*b*) outer areas of dormitory suburbs from which nearly everything that contributes to the well-being of a normal town is conspicuously absent".

Before the war the industrial development of Britain had, indeed, reached a chaotic and overbalanced condition. There was no rhyme nor reason in the way huge new factories sprang up along the by-passes and roads leading out of London, and along the outer rim of other large metropolises. Every aspect of common sense suggested that the time had come for a complete re-adjustment of factory development, but it took the general evolution of the war to create the circumstances under which a real change of policy could be put into effect.

In 1943 the Ministry of Town and Country Planning Act was introduced, by which central planning powers were transferred from the Ministry of Works and Buildings to a new Ministry charged with the duty of "ensuring consistency and continuity in the framing and execution of a national policy with respect to the use of the land". Several subsequent acts have created conditions under which the Government, in association with local authorities and industrial boards, is now endeavouring to re-plan Britain's industry on a regional basis. It is no use pretending that the Government's policy is entirely a satisfactory one, and it is probably too much to imagine that a policy of regionalization was initially responsible for the new trends. In fact, a British Government of to-day, whether Labour or Conservative, or Liberal, operates a basically centralized policy—in theory. Fortunately, the impact of practical events tends to adapt theories to actualities, and the trend of industrial development towards regionalization is a case in point. What Whitehall planners may often have inserted as face-saving clauses and conditions, have in many cases provided the facility for local initiative to extend and develop. Local authorities undoubtedly have lost some of their control to central Ministries—on the other hand they have gained access to financial resources which they have been able to put to good use for local benefit.

One of the first signs of a Government policy of regionalization has been the issue of various official planning reports covering most of the counties, conurbations, cities and towns. These cover the dispersal of population; road communications, including railways, docks, canals and airports; industry; housing; public and quasi-public buildings, e.g. schools, churches, etc.; public utility services; open spaces; and architecture and landscape. They make provision for the establishment of satellite towns; for industrial zoning according to the type of industry in question; for ring routes to avoid traffic congestion in the centres of large towns and for parkways to replace the old type of arterial roads; for at least seven acres of open space per thousand of the population; and for a new low density of housing.

In dealing with individual cities the plans are based on a conception of neighbourhood units of about 10,000 people, dove-tailing into districts of about five neighbourhood units, which in their turn dove-tail into the city as a whole. Since the passing of the New Town Acts, 1946, ten sites for New Town Development have been announced. Several of these towns are sited within a sixty-mile radius of London—Stevenage, Crawley-Three-Bridges, Hemel Hempstead, Marlow, Hatfield, Welwyn Garden City and Basildon. The others are Aycliffe and Easington (Peterlee), in County Durham; East Kilbride; and Glenrothes (an area of about 5,730 acres in the parishes of Markinch and Leslie) in Scotland.

Naturally a main feature of this new regional trend has been the development, or rather the re-development, of British industry. The Distribution of Industry Act of 1945 is now being applied actively to attract new industries to South Wales and Monmouthshire, the north-east coast, West Cumberland, industrial Scotland, Wrexham, South Lancashire, the Merseyside, and Inverness-shire.

When the war ended the Board of Trade took over the old "Special Area" companies, wholly financed by the Government, and with them the existing industrial estates, of which the most important were Treforest in South Wales, Team Valley at Gateshead and Hillington, near Glasgow. It was then decided to build a series of other new industrial estates on the same general plan in other parts of the areas where unemployment existed. Big Royal Ordnance factories and other new Government factories built during the war were converted to big-scale peacetime production instead of being allowed to go derelict as they had after the first war. Even the big filling factories which were technically difficult to use for peacetime work, were turned into new industrial estates for small firms, as a quick means of checking the immediate post-war rise in unemployment. Meantime, industrial estate companies, on behalf of the Government, set out to build in three years after the war a very large number of new factories in all parts of the areas where unemployment existed. Private firms were encouraged to build factories, not in congested areas like London and the south-east, but in the Development Areas.

By the end of 1949, 986 new factory buildings had been completed in the development areas. Unemployment was reduced from 932,000 in 1932 to 119,800 at mid-1949. Some 200,000 jobs have been provided by new factory development since 1945.

On the north-east coast, where the depression on Tyneside and south-west Durham had been a byword in pre-war years, unemployment has actually been reduced to 2.6 per cent., which was below Lord Beveridge's definition of full employment, the absolute minimum. In West Cumberland unemployment was down from the pre-war total of nearly 50 per cent. and upwards to $2\frac{1}{2}$ per cent. by June, 1949. In South Wales and Scotland, in parts of which the problem was peculiarly difficult the figure remained between 3 per cent. and 4 per cent.

In South Wales the Development Plan consisted, first of all, in the enlargement of the pre-war estate at Treforest, and the creation of three big new publicly-owned estates at Bridgend, Hirwaun, and Fforestfach near Swansea. At Treforest many new factories have been built since the war; and the estate is now probably the finest in the country, employing well over 10,000 factory workers. Bridgend in the Vale of Glamorgan, and Hirwaun right at the summit of the Aberdare Valley, in the very worst area of pre-war depression, were converted from wartime Royal Ordnance factories into industrial estates; and, despite the great difficulties this has involved, several thousand people are now employed by various light industries on each of these two estates. At Fforestfach, Swansea, where previously practically no light industry existed, ten large modern factories had been completed by the middle of 1949, and were in production, employing some 1,500 persons.

Almost every type of modern industry can be found on one or another of these four estates, including clothing, light engineering of all kinds, chemicals, toys, machinery, plastics, furniture, electrical equipment, food manufacture and so forth. Most of them are exporting a high proportion of their products. Secondly, the Government itself decided to continue its three new Royal Ordnance factories at Glascoed near Pontypool, at Cardiff, and at Pembrey in the far west of the area just beyond Llanelly. These have continued to produce munitions on a small scale, but have also successfully manufactured ordinary peacetime goods in general demand, including parts of Airey houses, ceramics, fertilizers (instead of explosives) and machinery.

Some very large new developments in the nation's basic industries have also been located in South Wales. Much the biggest of these are, first, the huge new steel works at Margam, worth about £60,000,000 and the biggest new industrial development in Europe; and, secondly, the new oil refineries at Llandarcy. In addition to these, a whole series of individual factories have been built, either by the Government or private enterprise in almost every part of the area. At Ponty-pool the finest nylon factory in Britain (begun in April, 1945) is now completed and in full production. In the Swansea Valley in West Wales a complete new watch industry is springing up in a group of modern factories built and owned by the Government, and under excellent working conditions. At Merthyr more than six full-scale modern factories have been built since the war, manufacturing toys, clothing, fully-fashioned stockings, household equipment, radios and other products.

In the Rhondda Valley and in the West Wales anthracite valleys, where the unemployment problem has proved most stubborn and difficult, factories have been built by the Government in advance of demand, some of them specially designed for employing silicotic ex-miners. Nearly all these factories have been let, and most of them are already in production. Altogether, by mid-1949 179 new factories had been completed in South Wales and a further seventy-four were being built.

On the north-east coast, by the middle of 1949 248 new factory buildings had been completed, and another forty-three building. Here, also, the pre-war estate at Team Valley has been greatly enlarged as well as the smaller pre-war estates at Sunderland and West Aukland; and a whole series of fine modern new estates have been located and built—at Jarrow (where twelve modern factories stand on a site which before the war was derelict wasteland), at West Chirton on North Tyneside, at Hartlepool, Middlesbrough and Stockton-on-Tees. Two wartime Royal Ordnance factories have also, as in South Wales, been converted into new industrial estates at Aycliffe, near Darlington (where a new town is now to be built) and at Spennymoor in the Durham coalfield. Both of these are employing several thousand persons, and produce a variety of engineering, clothing, chemical and other light and medium products. In addition, new development schemes in the iron and steel and chemical industries have also made great progress on the north-east coast. The most ambitious of these are the new steel and chemical schemes, both costing many millions, on the south bank of the Tees, near Middlesbrough.

Also on the north-east coast, a large number of individual projects have brought a series of new industries to districts hitherto wholly dependent on coal or steel, so ensuring a far better use of the national labour force. The biggest and most modern textile factory in Britain, for instance, has been built near Darlington; a very large new tobacco factory on North Tyneside; a number of new clothing factories in Hartlepool, Sunderland and South Shields; a furniture factory at West Chirton; several radio and engineering factories at Sunderland; an expanded mining machinery plant at Team Valley.

In West Cumberland, though the numbers involved are smaller, the transformation is perhaps even more spectacular. Unemployment has been almost wiped out by deliberate and careful planning, which has introduced a suitable new project into almost every part of the area. By the middle of 1949 as many as twenty-nine new factories had been built. There are small trading estates at Maryport and Workington; and a group of new factories at Whitehaven. Others are scattered in the villages themselves; and West Cumberland to-day produces children's clothes, light electrical goods, cosmetics, chemicals, woollen yarn and cloth, and a number of other products which were undreamt of before the war. In Workington itself there have been big modernization schemes in the historic iron and steel works and associated engineering plants. In the south of the area a wartime Royal Ordnance factory has been converted into one of the nation's principal atomic energy producing plants, for which West Cumberland's water supplies are particularly suitable.

Regionalization of industry has also increased in Scotland, where planners were confronted with the vast triple problem of Clydeside, of Lanarkshire, previously dependent only on coal and steel, and of Dundee, once almost wholly dependent on jute. All these areas were included in the Development Area under the 1945 Bill, and the Board of Trade set out to "steer" industrialists from the south (and also from the United States and elsewhere abroad) to these Scottish industrial areas. By mid-1949, already 290 new factory buildings had been completed and another 113 were still building. In addition to the original pre-war estate at Hillington, and three smaller Lanarkshire estates at Larkhall, Chapelhall and Carfin, a series of new ones was planned covering the whole area. By mid-1949 these were well on the way to completion at Dundee, Newhouse, Port Glasgow, Queenslie, Thornliebank, Vale of Leven, Kilwinning, Kilmarnock, Coatbridge, Carntyne and Blantyre. The Bishopton Royal Ordnance factory is continuing in production, and the Royal Ordnance factory at Cardonald has been converted into an industrial estate.

Individual industries of all kinds have come to Scotland. Amongst the biggest and most successful projects are: wool spinning and weaving, radio production, steel pressing, heavy electrical engineering, nuts and bolts, clock manufacture, and office machinery. In Dundee, in particular, a fine new industrial estate has been virtually completed, with a number of modern factories, which have brought a whole range of new work, including watch and clock making, to this city

149

which knew such extreme depression in the past.

As a result, unemployment has almost vanished from Dundee; and the menace of a possible depression in the jute trade has lost some of its force. Those who wish to see for themselves the success of the distribution of industry policy should visit the industrial estate at Dundee. At the same time throughout Lanarkshire, Clydeside, industrial Ayrshire and the Greenock area, new industries are steadily expanding. At Grangemouth, just outside the Development Area, one of Britain's great new oil refineries is being built.

So far I have described the more factual aspect of British industry's regional trend, an aspect directed and, so to speak, "prodded" by the Government. Socially and culturally, too, the results are bound to reflect a much healthier sort of life, with people given the room and space to develop their local activities.

Naturally, in all this regional industrial development, it is unavoidable that a certain amount of upheaval of domestic life has been occasioned. This is glossed over in the official Government accounts, but it must be faced up to and admitted. There is a natural antipathy on the part of most human beings to being uprooted from their familiar surroundings—even if these are the over-crowded slums of a city—and planted down in a new and strange background. This was evidenced during the war, when a percentage of evacuated people inevitably returned to their homes and the bombs, rather than face a new life. Yet, as against that, another percentage so much liked the new life that they stayed and settled permanently. It is probably true to say that the objection to transfer from city to less over-crowded areas is more the objection to *compulsion* as such than to actual transfer of background. Otherwise why has there been an immense movement away from the cities, back to the land, immigration and so forth?

Some idea of how this human problem has been approached was given by Dennis H. Morgan, Location Officer for Wales for the Board of Trade, in an address on "The Changing Face of South Wales" to members of the Cardiff Naturalists' Society. Referring to the expansion of new industries in Welsh development areas, he said:

"The establishment of a new business, or a branch of a business, must inevitably involve the transfer of at least a few key workers and the visiting industrialist is compelled to look through the eyes of his key workers *and* of their wives and families, at the districts which they are to adopt as their future homes. Will they be prepared to leave their own villas in one of the suburbs of London or Birmingham to accept a council house in say the Rhondda, Merthyr, Maesteg or Gorseinon?

"The local authorities in the main, are co-operating with us, allocating a percentage of their newly-built houses for the use of imported key workers and we are thus hoping that the housing problem will be largely overcome. But these folk will be coming to what is regarded by them as a 'foreign country' and a heavy responsibility rests upon the people in the districts where factories are to be erected to make these new-comers feel at home as rapidly as possible. In these valley towns there are many cultural and social activities; our new friends must be made welcome into these activities so that they may be compensated for the loss of the social contacts which have been severed in their former home districts. In the case of directors and employees of managerial grades, steps are being taken by the Estate Company on behalf of the Board of Trade to erect houses of somewhat larger dimensions than those of the normal council house and we have already received applications for over 300 of these houses.

"I was recently talking to a man who had been sent by his firm to manage its new factory in Wales and he told me that he had been warned by a Welsh friend in London that, on arrival, he should immediately start a Works Choir, join the Chapel and become a vice-president of the local Rugger Club! That may be an exaggeration but it recognizes the need for an understanding of the

Welsh temperament and it is up to us to recipro-
cate. I do not suggest that these firms and their
key workers are coming to us from merely philan-
thropic motives—but their coming will mean very
much to us and we should do all in our power to
make them welcome."

This human side of the industrial world is
particularly important in the regional areas.
In London and perhaps one or two of the big
cities, industrial workers are often able to divide
their lives into two worlds—the factory at which
they spend a certain ordained period of the day,
and their home life, which is quite divorced from
the working life (especially as in many cases they
travel some distance from home to work). In the
regional areas, however, the life of the factory is
often bound up intimately with the social life.
This trend was emphasized during the war, when
in many large-scale industries—engineering, syn-
thetics, chemicals, armaments—the workers lived
either in the immediate vicinity of the factories,
or actually in adjoining hostels. The tendency
has continued, and is one upon whose effect—for
good or bad—it is difficult to pronounce. Mass-
production in itself has a de-vitalizing, de-huma-
nizing effect upon the individual and undoubtedly
most of our large-scale industries are organized
on mass-production lines. If people are already
merely cogs in a machine, and then proceed to
identify their outside life increasingly with the

same machine, then the prospect seems to me a bleak one. If, however, the work of the industry is more intimately associated with the local background—as, for instance, coal-mining might be, or the making of china clay (as in Cornwall) or of furniture (as at High Wycombe)—then the position is a healthier one. The best hope for industries that have set up in new areas is that they may gradually make for themselves a place in the local pattern of life, taking on some of the attributes and characteristics of the locality, finally identifying themselves and acquiring a local pride. I believe the policy of many industrialists is to encourage such a trend, and it is one to be applauded.

This industrial regionalization, at which I can only hint in this short chapter, is of immense importance to the British nation. If continued with—and there is every indication that no matter what party is in power, de-centralization is a set policy—this steady redistributing out of population and industries will produce a much less chaotic pattern of life. If factories we must have, then what a difference between a model factory in some beautiful country setting, and the old type of ugly, misshapen, smoky deathtrap buried among city streets. Not only employees but employers to-day are agreed upon the improvements, in work, health and happiness, resulting from the re-planning of industries upon a regional basis. Some of our industries must remain in and around the big cities; it is too late now to go back on the follies of our ancestors. But even they will benefit from the fact that no new factories will be allowed to develop beside them.

I have said nothing about agriculture, because to talk of the regional trend in agriculture would be superfluous. In agriculture one sees the basis and justification for the regional life. A healthy agriculture, which is now recognized as essential to Britain's prosperity, is every nation's Number One industry. With agriculture as a basis, local industries and crafts grow up naturally, together with their own social and cultural life. The result is a continuous pattern; the regional life. On the land we build our life, and from the land we derive our life. And the land is never more fertile and beautiful than when it is green and growing, never more grey and lifeless than when it is buried beneath the weight of stone pavements and city buildings.

CRAFTS

THE war hit British craftsmanship hard. Out of some 2,000 or so craftsmen of pre-war days (excluding rural crafts) there were at one time during the war fewer than twenty workshops left. At the time this might not have seemed a potential disaster, but looking back now from the security of peace we realize what a tragedy was narrowly averted. Craftsmanship depends upon an abundance of time; it is not something that can be put on and off like a convenient coat. Anyone can knock a rivet into a metal part, but not anyone can weave a cloth or shape a pot. Craftsmanship has been described as the gradual transfer of the bodily knowledge of the right usage of material and the intimate co-operation of small groups of workers. If the continuity is broken, and the workers and their materials split up, then not only is a craft lost—but a whole heritage.

It is difficult for a layman to convey the subtleties of craftsmanship, yet it is important to do so for those subtleties mark an immense gap that separates the craftsman from the industrial worker. When I wrote in the previous chapter of the regional trend of industry I was dealing with something "on the surface" compared to crafts.

Industry is new and raw, in comparison to the craftsmanship from which it has sprung. In a way the results of industrialization may be described as a symbolic measure of the mistake mankind has made in spurning crafts for quantities. Leon Bloy once offered a large sum of money to anyone who could prove to him that there was a greater folly than travelling over the ground at fifty miles an hour. In the same spirit it is relevant to inquire why it is considered an advantage to be able to produce one hundred synthetic products that will last a year or two as compared to half a dozen of the same that will last a lifetime. The only justification—and of course it is constantly presented as an irrefutable argument—is the urgency of the moment. People *must* have houses, therefore it is better to give them metal huts and other temporary buildings than to build for them the solid, craftsman's houses such as our ancestors favoured. People *must* have smart new clothes, therefore these must be run off on mass-production machines, rather than individually fashioned by craftsmen and women, as in the past. There is only one honest view to take of craftsmanship, and that is—it represents the best. In every instance where we accept the inferior mass-produced articles, we are in fact helping to transform ourselves into inferior people.

That, as I say, is the idealistic view. One of

Britain's greatest craftsmen, Bernard Leach, the potter, has summed up his feeling on the matter in a pamphlet on *My Work as Potter*.

"Craftsmanship in its essence is the antidote of mass-production, and the craftsman is the residual type of fully responsible workman. The educated craftsman ever since the time of Morris and Ruskin, let us say from about the middle of last century, has by force of circumstance, been more or less of an artist, that is to say, he had often received previous training as an artist, or as an architect. He follows a craft as a vocation for the enthusiasm of the thing made by hand to the best of man's ability. Whether it be pot or poem, painting, music or sculpture, the type of man and his processes of thought are much the same. The social circumstances which have thrown him up as a reactionary against the over-mechanization of labour at a certain stage following the Industrial Revolution, have been similar in all modern countries. This kind of man or woman is possessed of an insight into the epochs of man's culture and in his or her own workshop passes such influences through the mesh of personality.

"Our problem is to preserve those qualities of concept, of material and of method, belonging to pre-industrial civilization which are still valid to-day, adding to them an individual responsibility and a width of outlook which is our peculiar Western inheritance. This constant straining after perfection in the thing made may either continue alongside industry, as a stimulus and example, or it may serve within the factory to redeem it from sheer commercialism.

"We in England are the parents of industrialism. As such we have had more time to observe the effects of mechanization and to begin to take its measure. It is but just that the evils inherent in the misuse of science should be understood and countered first by us. All over the East, all over the world, in fact, the same thing is, or has been, taking place. Broadly, the same sequence of events follows close upon the establishment of factories or the large-scale importation of mass-produced goods; local handicrafts are displaced, the close contacts between maker and consumer. between heart and hand, man and material, art and life, all these are forgotten or lost in a very few years. The fabric of life is torn, faith weakens, culture itself—the soul of a people—disintegrates.

"The artist-craftsman should be the natural source of contemporary applied design, whether he works in conjunction with industry or prefers, as most of us do, to carry out our ideas in clay, cotton, wood, glass, metal or leather, etc., mainly with our own hands and at our own tempo. The hand is the prime tool and it expresses human feelings intimately; the machine for quantity, cheapness, and, at best, a marvellous efficiency, but it turns man into a modern slave unless it is counterbalanced by work which springs from the heart and gives form to the human imagination."

It would be difficult to imagine an industrialist speaking or thinking in such terms. Industrialist-philosophers there are, but their thoughts dwell upon facts and figures, higher output, greater production facilities—more and more, bigger and bigger, better and better. Unhappily, the adjectives do not always go together. "The hand is the prime tool and it expresses feelings intimately"—how more humble, and yet somehow more satisfying, are the words of Bernard Leach.

Craftsmanship, then, is still with us, a living thing, spreading its tentacles, however precariously, throughout the land. And indeed, that is one of its greatest merits—that it is almost entirely rural rather than urban—that its roots spread far and deep, rather than coil up in the shallow rootless worlds of the cities. There is little need to consider the question of a redistribution of crafts. They have distributed themselves very well—from the Harris tweed workers of Scotland to the paper-makers of Somerset, the lace-makers of Nottingham to the stone hewers of the Isle of Purbeck, in Dorset. Most crafts have continued down a period of centuries, carrying on traditions that go back to the beginning of the history books. The potters of to-day differ only in style and design from potters of thousands of years ago (only the other day a walker on Land's End found a beaker dating back more than two thousand years).

To-day, Britain's crafts are not only reviving but expanding, aided now by a more enlightened Government attitude. The first efforts for this expansion, however, had to be made by the craftsmen themselves. It is symbolized by a new organization, the British Craft Association of Great Britain, which has a large membership and exhibition rooms in London—and also organizes important shows in America and elsewhere that produce export orders running into tens of thousands of pounds. It is the ultimate idea that craft centres should be established in every region of the British Isles.

Crafts in the regions are also helped through such bodies as the Rural Industries Bureau, which are organized county by county. One of the Bureau's many services is the provision of financial aid to enable craftsmen to repair or renew their equipment. Surveys are also carried out. One such survey in the West Country revealed that there were no fewer than 400 separate crafts being pursued. These included pottery, wrought-iron work, embroidery, basket-making, copper-beating, printing, leathercraft, sculpture, heraldry, shellcraft, knitwear, jewellery, stool making. What is happening in the west is happening in many other parts. In Glamorgan, for instance, there are numerous rural crafts in operation—

blacksmiths, wheelwrights, saddlers, thatchers, potters, coopers. The same can be said of Scotland and Northern Ireland.

The crafts of Britain are essentially regional because they have arisen, in very many cases, out of the geographical nature of their background. What could be more natural than that a craft of stone-carving should develop in the Isle of Purbeck, where is quarried some of the finest stone in the country? Where a more natural home for tweed-making than the island of Lewis, where the tweeds are dried in sweet dry winds such as probably exist nowhere else in the British Isles? How sensible and practical that hand-made pottery should be a major craft in Cornwall (there are at least a dozen established potteries in the county) where is mined the china clay so necessary for the making of pots.

In each case these local crafts have developed as an integral part of a pattern of local life, often becoming so woven into that pattern that it is difficult to separate the craft from the life. A maker of hand-beaten copper, Francis Cargeeg, has written about this aspect, showing how, as a Celt himself, he felt a curious, almost instinctive interest in the work of the ancient Celtic craftsmen, in the creativity of a race whose dominion stretched for a thousand years from the Black Sea to the western coast of Ireland.

"Its artists in pottery, weaving, metal-work,

enamelling, ecclesiastical stonework and illuminated manuscripts gave to Europe a masterly abstract art of curvilinear and geometric ornament. They excelled, however, in metalwork; and in hammered sheet bronze, which is copper with a little tin added, they found a medium that perfectly suited their instincts and achieved astonishing results in the technique of 'embossing' designs which we now know as 'repoussé'. Their designs were drawn by the flow of light on polished metal, which gave an elusive beauty to their oft-times flamboyant and bizarre forms.

"My interests thus led inevitably to Celtic metalwork, and to hammered copper as an ideal medium to interpret the spirit which lived in the scrolls, the spiral and trumpet 'motifs' and the amazing patterns of knot-work so beloved by the ancient artist-craftsman."

Cargeeg's art is one that had dwindled in this country, but that is now showing signs of revival. It is essentially a craft of the people, for the time is not so very distant when almost every country cottage could boast a gleaming copper kettle, copper trays and other utensils whose glow brought an added warmth and beauty into the home. At the same time it is a craft that can touch the highest peaks of artistry. As Cargeeg has written:

"My own aim has always been to make the ornament an integral part of the shape and let it grow out of it, so that there is an uninterrupted play of light over the whole surface, and not, as has been the tendency at the art schools, to treat the ornament as something to be put on. It is the flow of light, its elusive moulding of the shape and design, the rich warm colour of a lovely metal, that are the gifts of my art.

"My tribute has been by hand, hammer and fire to make a living reality of a great traditional art. My experience has brought me an acute sense of fellowship with my forerunners and a satisfaction in sharing in the significant and inevitable revival of the crafts. Significant, because it is part of that questing for those basic aesthetic values, which hag-ridden by the analytical spirit of a scientific age, the artist bewilderingly seeks. Inevitable, because all they seek has been part of the way of life, labour and thought of artist-craftsmen since the dawn-cultures of mankind. Hence the haunting of the studios, the hopeful drawing together of the artist and the craftsman, and the emergence of the artist-craftsman of a new age."

It is interesting to note here yet another expression of the idea that crafts are in the hands of artists. This is undoubtedly the modern trend of thought, and there is perhaps a danger of the slightly detached "artist-conception" shifting the emphasis too much from the basic idea of hand-toil-labour suggested by the word craft. On the other hand, the change seems inevitable in an age when most roots with the past have been broken, and the task is to revive and re-establish craftsmanship on a plane that has meaning for generations who do not understand the traditional background of the old craftsmen. It is this fact, I feel, that justifies the appearance of so many exhibitions and displays of craftsmanship, whereas in the old days there would have been no such organized displays, since the articles themselves would have been in as much daily use as cups and saucers, books and bread. Craftsmen have the big task of educating, or perhaps re-educating, the people of Britain to an understanding of their heritage.

This aspect of the craftsman's new task has been well expressed by Archibald Carne, one of Britain's foremost makers of wrought-iron work. He says that the customer dropping in at the forge with a problem in furnishing a home, the architect who presents a specific and detailed order, the letter with a general query of possibility and price—all set forth a living demand from their different approaches.

"It is a demand of intriguing variety, from the restoration of an Adam grate to the repairing of a suit of armour, from the simple domestic light fitting to massive ornamental gates. Meeting each as it comes with drawing and finished piece, trying to satisfy the client and his own ideas and standards at the same time, the craftsman makes his contribution according to his powers, towards the re-establishment of his craft in a changing world."

At the forges of craftsmen like Carne, parties of students from local senior schools come for instruction, while he himself travels to give talks and demonstrations to schools, art societies and other groups. This is a development of immense potential importance to the craft movement, a replacement of the old apprentice system by a more general educational propaganda—that may bring back, eventually, the apprentice. Not that, in general, there is any shortage of students for crafts. Whereas there are complaints of lack of trainees for such admittedly unattractive occupations as coal-mining, many of the crafts report a positive embarrassment of students. At technical colleges all over the country principals report a steady increase in attendances for courses of printing, pottery, embroidery, woodwork, engraving, etc. At one of England's leading hand-made potteries, equipped for employing about twenty full-time workers, there is a waiting list of nearly 400 people who want to come and work there.

At this pottery, and at many other crafts establishments—such as the several maintained at Dartington Hall, Devon, or the Gill printing works near High Wycombe, the crafts carried on

by the Society of Brothers, near Ludlow, or by
the monks of Buckfast Abbey—the craft is the hub
of a way of life. Both responsibilities and profits
are shared so far as possible, but not dogmatically
—each doing what he is best fitted to do, and to
the extent of which he is capable. In some cases
there may be a religious belief holding together
the members of a craft centre, in others the bond
may be a simple joy and delight in the work done.
Time after time one hears of people whose lives
have been cut adrift by the war, feeling somehow
that there is something wrong and arid about the
modern industrialized way of life—and finding
in some ancient craft a creative satisfaction which
redirects their whole lives.

In this process, they are merely experiencing,
and expressing intellectually, what has been felt
by craftsmen down all the ages, whether they be
the craftsmen of stone or clay, of wood or copper,
of the paint-brush or of the spade. In effect they
are rejoining a mainstream of continuous experience, whose nature is at once emphasized by,
and dependent upon, its continuity. A well-
known hand-printer, Guido Morris, has made
this point well, when commenting about paper.
Modern machine-made paper, he says, is beautiful
and consistent, but *it has relatively no character.*
Hand-made paper is full of character: and in
mills where the same families for generations
have employed the same families of workers,

there must be an atmosphere of friendship inseparable from the feeling of the paper they make.

In the past the family continuity was a basic part of most crafts, and one thinks even to-day with pleasure of such craftsmen-families as the Dolmetsch's (harpsichords), the Leach's (pottery) and the Nance's (furniture)—there are many more, of course. It is to be hoped that this family tradition continues to exist, but obviously it has been disturbed by the intrusion of the Industrial Revolution, political upheavals, wars and other outside events. Fortunately, a rigidly family succession is not necessarily vital to the continuation of crafts. A blacksmith once described to me how he was born not of a family of craftsmen—but born in the country, in a world of horses and carts, ploughs and harrows. To watch half a dozen or more big steaming horses waiting to be shod in the light of the forge fire, while the smith worked merrily and commandingly with red-hot bars of iron, was a thrill. He began "dropping in" again and again whenever school and odd jobs allowed, and the ambition inevitably grew to be a smith. Schooldays over, he was apprenticed, and has never regretted it.

It may not always be as simple as that, but the opportunity will always be there. It is an opportunity that lies waiting in every region, and one which is being taken up by an increasing number of young people. The reasons which prompt them in this direction are often superficially quite different, yet at the bottom they have a unity of purpose. It is the urge to create, and above all to create directly. Contact: it is the eternal loss of the machine worker, the eternal secret of the craftsman. The craftsman is *the fully responsible* workman. He is responsible because he alone can make or mar the quality of his work—in his hands only can it come to life, or death.

"My work is already ancient when it leaves my hands. I believe it has always been buried in me and in the stone," writes Sven Berlin, the sculptor, in his book *Disturbance in the West*. "From having the potentiality of many different shapes it is revealed finally in a crystallization of these in the only way it could have been done. . . . The artist submits entirely to the law and drive of his inner life and to the law of the stone, its grain, tension, gravity and strength. He becomes an instrument through which these two sets of natural laws are co-operating, rather than conflicting, to find a union in the created image, potential in the moment between all these forces.

"He is not, therefore, working in a state of conscious will, using his intellect alone, but with it he is using his physique, instinct, emotion and unconscious mental force, from which emanates his experience of the whole drama of human life. It is precisely this union of the worlds through

169

the material that explains the paradox of un-reasonability and illuminates our understanding through more senses than one.

"In this way he is enabled to be *in* the stone yet looking at the image—which is also within himself—from many points of view at one time. The stone becomes a valley, a mountain, a twisted road; it is the curve of the falling wave, a dance, a journey to the stars. All these experiences are lived out in submission to a poetic idea, which, when it is made concrete, is something grown out of the fusion of objective, mental and plastic fantasy, made to live in space by the mysterious force we call creative energy, the source of which we know nothing."

And so another craftsman attempts to explain the miracle of craftsmanship, of creation. There is no final explanation, but the true craftsman is always searching for it in words—while making it with materials. If this country of ours could only be turned increasingly into the custody of such questing, imaginative, responsible hands, it would be a much better land—and we much better people.

THE MEANING OF REGIONALISM

THE aim of this short book has been to give a factual picture of the new regional trend of social and cultural life in Britain, sketching in the background and illustrating what has been achieved so far. If my approach has been somewhat uncritical, that has been for the good reason that it is important, first, to demonstrate that there *is* a regional renaissance. It would be possible to go into greater detail, to give further instances of how people all over the country are beginning to turn inwards, into the reality of their own local life, rather than outwards to the unreality of a synthetic life outside their physical awareness. At the same time, it would be possible to criticize many aspects of this new regionalism. It faces the inevitable danger of becoming a cult. Although regionalism is not anything new in itself, to many people it appears as something new. Consequently they eulogize it, rhapsodize about the benefits of the new life away from the smoky deprivations of the cities. Personally I am in favour of a country life, but I do not think it would be fair to identify regionalism with rurlism. A region is an area, a natural "whole" constituted by many smaller parts—in short, a small country. And every country is made up of towns as well as villages, rows of houses as well as scattered cottages. Indeed towns, as much as villages, contribute to the over-all character of a region. Wales is as much the Wales of Cardiff and Caernarvon, Llanelly and Llandudno, as it is the Wales of Cader Idris, Bala Lake and the Pembroke coast. Scotland would hardly be Scotland without Edinburgh—Ulster not properly Ulster without Belfast. And the West Country would not seem the same without such deep-rooted centres as Dorchester, Salisbury, Bristol and Bath. It was of Bath that Swinburne once wrote:

> Like a queen enchanted, that may not laugh or weep,
> Glad at heart and guarded from change and care
> like ours,
> Girt about with beauty by days and nights that creep
> Soft as breathless ripples that softly shoreward sweep,
> Lies the lovely city, whose grace no grief deflowers.

Bath would serve very well as the perfect example of an alive provincial town (or, in this case, city), with its graceful curving side streets, its delightful architecture—its old squares and churches, terraces and crescents—its Pump Room, Roman Baths, Assembly Rooms, parks and parades, theatres—the annual Bath Festival of the Arts. I have only visited Bath, but even to a visitor it conveys an atmosphere of peace and culture, of life savoured as it should be, leisurely and with taste.

Other cities differ, of course. It would be difficult to find somewhere less like Bath than, say, Birmingham, that depressing testimonial to industrialism run riot. Yet this city faithfully reflects the character of its region, and if inspected and experienced thoroughly will be found rich in kindness and humour, strength and courage, in that frankness that belongs to the Midlands. Its tragedy is that the good, wholesome kernel has been swamped by the fringes—just as, on a much vaster scale, suburbia has killed London. The London of two hundred years ago, or of further back—of Shakespeare's time, perhaps— that was a London full of richness and character. Even later, in the times of Dickens and of Turner, reading the lives of those eminent men, one gets a picture of London that is vastly more vivid and colourful than to-day.

But isn't it mere wishful thinking to imagine that our towns and cities were better places before industrialization? Quite possibly: we know from a study of social history what conditions of filth and misery existed in the past. To-day our cities and towns, in particular, have the most up-to-date aids of medicine and science. Hospitals and health clinics are available to give immediate treatment —to what? To a list of ailments, *a very large percentage of which* are due to the mere fact of existing in crowded, intensely built-up areas whose sky-lines are dominated by smoke from factories, whose daily life is active with noise and nervous tension. Any doctor can confirm this. The Ministry of Health will confirm it—they have issued some fascinating statistics about the change in health of orphan children switched from London homes, to encampments in the country. The improvement in health was de-scribed as "unbelievable".

A case for country living, then? In many ways —but not without qualification. Most things in life would be very much better if we could wipe the slate clean and start afresh. Or so we like to think. In practice, we often find that there is some reason, some necessity of experience, behind every development. It may be that the experience of industrialized city life has been a necessity—just as some would say wars have been a necessity—if only to demonstrate very precisely why a mass of society concentrated almost entirely in a few large cities is a danger to the future of the nation.

Why is it a danger? The quickest answer to that is, look at London. Look at Glasgow. A better answer is to examine the over-all shape of Britain, the distribution of its population—to reflect upon that astonishing fact that until recently nearly 80 per cent. of the population of this country resided in London, Birmingham,

Manchester, Merseyside, Tyneside, West Yorkshire and Glasgow. If one were to discover an apple tree with 80 per cent. of the apples clustered together along four or five out of its many branches—that would be a visual example of the effect of our present distribution of population. I am not an agricultural expert but I should be very surprised to find that such an apple tree would be regarded as being in a healthy condition. Perversion and distortion—they have been twin faults of this age. Building without foundations, concentrating instead of spreading out, centralizing control instead of distributing it—they are all distortions of the natural development of ourselves and our lives. One has seen in such contemporary sports as football how the fashion for glamorizing the individual has caused untold harm. And one has seen, too, how real teamwork has again and again achieved victory in the face of individual showmanship.

With that admission, that the whole is more important than the individual—at least in the material sense—we come to a consideration of regionalism in itself. Is it justified? Is it not putting the clock back to try and go back on our tracks? But, of course, there is no chance of going back on our tracks. They have, in fact, been obliterated by time and so-called progress. We cannot raise the dead, but we do not need to blaspheme them. If we are not prepared to learn

and benefit from the experiences of thousands of
years of human life, then we are indeed adrift and
rootless and on the way to extermination. But
if we are so prepared, then we must see that
throughout the ages mankind has sought, above
all, *roots*. A background, a home, an identity—
someone and somewhere to belong to—surely the
desire for these is inbred in us all? If we assume
the family as the backbone of society (in these
days a fact so uncertain has, unfortunately, to be
assumed) we have a vision of the world spread
out among hundreds of millions of units. That is
our first identity, one of a family unit. Next
comes the identity of being one of a group of
families, and then of a larger group of families,
and so on. Test this in your own life. The everyday circumstances that most immediately affect
you are those around you: home, work, play,
hobbies, meeting with other people. You are less
affected, at the moment, by what happens beyond the horizon, in another country—even in
another part of your own country. In the long
run you might very well be affected by these
distant happenings, but not in the present moment.
In the present moment the world is you, and all
of which you are physically, mentally and visibly
aware.

Regionalism is merely a crystallization of this
obvious fact. In effect it is a half-way house, a
compromise. True regionalism would return the

power, and therefore the responsibility, to the smallest possible units of individuals—possibly to the village, which would correspond to the tribe of ancient times. I always like to remember a story of the parish council of a tiny Cornish village— I think it was Mousehole—holding a special meeting upon the outbreak of the 1914-18 war, and after duly deliberating the situation, declaring the village "neutral". The days when such powers really lay in the hands of responsible individuals in a locality are long since gone. Not only villages, but counties, regions, whole countries are committed to treaties, responsibilities— wars even—without any real say on the part of the individuals. In the village where I live, no man can build even a hut in his garden without filling up several forms and dispatching them to some remote authority nearly two hundred miles away. It is possible, unless one is waiting for some wood with which to build a hut, to take a detached view and understand that rationing is imposed to prevent the few taking unfair advantage of the many. But such an understanding cannot alter the cold hard fact that abstract restrictions may tend, and are already tending, to devitalize initiative, to take away from perfectly worthy citizens their sense of responsibility.

"Where two nations, one large and one small, are ruled by the same Government it is not sufficiently realized that the power of the Government over the small nation is such that its apathy can be as effective as armaments in destroying it."

Those words from an article on Wales by Gwynfor Evans, president of the Welsh Nationalist Party, might apply equally well to the centralized government of a region. They apply especially to Wales, a country which, as Mr. Evans puts it, will have to fight furiously for any kind of decentralization. And yet Wales is a nation, historically and geographically. Why should its fate be decided by "a group of gentlemen sitting in London", as Mr. Aneurin Bevan put it before he joined them himself?

"No country can be said to be free and responsible unless it can choose its national policy. The policy for Wales should be decided by the people of Wales. This is impossible without a Welsh Parliament and Government. Issues far weightier than the fate of Wales absorb the time and interest of the present Parliament, where the Welsh members are a passive minority of 8 per cent. Welsh distress is too desperate to be removed by a mere administrative authority which leaves the seat of effective power where it is. The true remedy involves a radical constitutional change. It lies in the election of a Parliament for Wales and the creation of a Welsh democratic State. That alone can remove the frustration of the long years of vain agitation for such elementary necessities as a road through Wales. A Welsh Government alone can prevent the deportation of Welshmen from their homes and country; it alone can prevent the bargaining away of Welsh markets, can foster Welsh agriculture, develop the vast potentialities of our coal and other mineral deposits, and establish light industries throughout the country. Only a Welsh Government can give its whole time to the reconstruction of Wales. For every minute the present Parliament gives Wales, the Welsh Parliament would give a month.

"Democracy would thus become a greater reality in Wales. The Government would be brought nearer to the people, whose whole life would be stimulated by the supreme adventure of rebuilding their national life from its foundations. Having a more effective voice in the government, their interests could no longer be flouted with impunity."

What is said of Wales can equally be said of Scotland, which also lacks a government and parliament of its own, though it does at least boast a Secretary of State. It is increasingly difficult for the Scottish people to be persuaded that it is to their advantage to be absorbed into the economy of England. The reaction against this unnecessary domination takes the form of a revival of Scottish national literature and art, of crafts and customs, of the Scots and Gaelic and

Lallans languages. The same trend is noticeable in Eire, where the Gaelic tongue is being steadily revived. Even in Cornwall, another Celtic country, more and more people are taking up the study of the Cornish language. The motive behind this trend has been well expressed by R. W. Crombie Saunders, editor of *Scottish Art and Letters:* "We are beginning to realize that the dilemma of belonging to one race whilst trying to express ourselves in the language of another is as intolerable as pretending that our needs, our aims and our standards should be the same."

What has been said about Wales and Scotland is applicable to the various regions of England. Gwynfor Evans is right when he insists that the real and greatest obstacle to self-government is a passion for huge units of government. This megalomania springs from thinking of politics in terms of power rather than in terms of welfare.

"Wales has the inestimable advantage of being small enough to be properly governed. For some reason this is often considered a liability. It is our greatest asset. After examining five of the most successful States in the world, Sir E. D. Simon, in *The Smaller Democracies*, says that their small size is their great advantage. 'I have pointed out over and over again,' he says, 'the comparative ease of managing a small population as against the difficult world-wide problems of a country like Great Britain.' "

I do not wish to spend time here on the issue of nationalism, except to emphasize that nationalism in itself can be a good and creative thing. Opponents of nationalism really mean, in their attacks, *bad* nationalism, the sort displayed by Nazi Germany and, in certain aspects, by America and Russia to-day. On the other hand, a creative sort of nationalism, pride in one's national race and background, one's cultural heritage, language achievements—this is merely an extension of pride in oneself and one's abilities. And surely that is not a bad thing?

When the subject is approached from this angle it is extremely difficult to disagree with people like Mr. Evans, or with suggestions that small nations like Wales should be granted their own government. To-day the Labour Government are against such a development, but in 1918 one of the leaders, Arthur Henderson, urged such a policy:

"All the problems that embarrass statesmen and challenge the imagination of reformers are to be seen in Wales reduced to manageable proportions. Given self-government Wales might establish itself as a modern Utopia, and develop its own initiative, its own arts, its own national culture, its ideal of democracy in politics, industry and social life, as an example and an inspiration to the rest of the world."

And it was none other than Ramsay Mac-

Donald who said that "one of the most important measures of reconstruction after the war should be national self-determination within this kingdom".

Both statesmen were referring to small nations, such as Wales. And yet how easily their words can be applied to the regions, too. The north of England may not have a language of its own, but it has very little to connect it with, say, the West Country. Even within a region, such as the west, there is an infinite variety of character and outlook. Sometimes the differences can reach such proportions, as in the case of Cornwall, that one county can seem a world apart from others. There were several grains of common sense contained in the joke of a recent Free Cornwall movement, publicized in the national press: notably, the fact that Cornwall, if an independent unit, could be very much better off economically than now (when her fish hauls and broccoli crops may well be ruined through some Whitehall administrative decision to import Norwegian fish and Italian broccoli).

To-day, carried to excess, ideas of de-centralization might become inefficient and chaotic (though they might do us all a lot of good as individuals). It may be too late now to go back to village councils and so forth. But it is not too late to intensify a broad regionalization of this country. It is unfortunate that the initiative for the movement must still, in many cases, come from the very central authority which is its greatest enemy. For me, at any rate, half of the value of the Arts Council is nullified by the fact that it is, basically, a London-controlled concern with London ideas and London officials. Nevertheless I try to remember—and this is something we should all remember—that the money which the Arts Council spends comes from the taxpayer, you and me. It is therefore our privilege, and responsibility, to do all we can to see that at least a fair amount of the money is spent in our own locality. The same with developments of the Ministry of Works, the Ministry of Education, the Ministry of Town and Country Planning, all those apparently remote and untouchable Government departments. They are ultimately responsible to you and me.

The trouble is that when one reads such a sentence again, its emptiness becomes apparent. We can no longer really believe in it, because we can no longer establish the fact with our own eyes. We cannot really believe that we are able to exert an influence on the Ministry of This or That, because for all we know, they might not exist at all. And when occasionally we come upon some of their representatives, travelling educational inspectors or travelling planners of the Ministry of Works, we cannot really take them seriously. For if we do, and ask them some pertinent questions, they inevitably retire behind the bland defence of reference to "a higher authority", or some such code expression.

How different if every Government department was humanized in the shape of that provincial newspaper editor described by W. L. Andrews, editor of the *Yorkshire Post*:

"He cannot walk down the High Street of his own town without being saluted and buttonholed. . . . . What is the effect of this daily neighbourly pressure, reinforced by letters from readers telling of mistakes in the paper— for all of which the editor is blamed? He is kept under a wholesome discipline by his public, and is bound to be zealous for accuracy and proportion. . . ."

There is the case for a more independent regionalization free of the somehow suspect encouragement of centralized Government. One cannot help feeling that the local man who starts his own local business, employing local workers and manufacturing local products, or materials using some local products, is more genuine than some detached "firm" who, at the blandishments of a London Ministry, condescend to build their new factory not on the outskirts of London but in some remote valley of Wales. In the same way, one would wish for each region to be really free to govern itself—instead of, as is the case with our modern county councils, being hamstrung on all sides by various Government regulations.

In short, freedom should be total rather than conditional, earned rather than handed out from a "higher authority". If we have to recognize that such is unlikely to be the case, that the Mousehole declaration of "neutrality" is more a gesture than a fact, we can still work with all our power towards the maximum amount of regional development. If we cannot rule our own regions, then we can at least exert our maximum influence upon the ruling. If we cannot conveniently obliterate our existing industrial eyesores and over-crowded towns, let us at least concentrate our energies on de-horrifying them. And if we must accept a good deal of centralized financial aid and direction in the development of local cultural efforts, especially in regard to the building of suitable premises—let us make sure that we fill the buildings with a maximum amount of local culture (do not, for instance, let us lose to oblivion a Thomas Hardy for the sake of an Irving Berlin, or even for a French painter or a German musician).

In our schools let us make sure that children learn the reality of the life around them, as well as the equal yet different reality of the worlds beyond their sight. In our work, let us encourage the craftsman before the shift-server, the maker before the middleman. In our social life let us seek our contacts and our companionship, our mental and physical stimulation, from the people among whom we belong—the people next door, the people across the street, the people in the next road and the next village.

After all, we have one immense—I believe unconquerable—advantage on our side. We are the majority. The fact that until recently 80 per cent. of the population was resident in the great industrialized areas and cities does not mean they chose that way of life. Far from it: economic necessity and that alone has put most of these people where they are. Even so they are constantly restless, a feeling expressed by the steady stream of immigrations, of "back to the land" adventures. Ironically enough, the same "economic necessity" that has lumped everyone together seems likely now to contribute to spacing them out (redistribution of industries, etc.). This will bring a surge of new life and blood to some of the more starved regions, causing a stimulus that may well carry the new regionalism to new heights.

The regional renaissance has begun. Its progress will always be slow and steady, rather than dramatic. In that, it corresponds to most natural growths. From the point of view of the satiated reader of "hot" news, there is something most undramatic in the story of a man planting the seed of a tree which will not grow to full stature for perhaps a hundred years. Yet from another point of view, such an act is immensely dramatic, containing in itself all the great elements of the drama of life and death. I know a man whose ambition is to spend the rest of his life planting trees up and down the tiny valleys of a stretch of English coastline. The fact that he will be dead fifty years before they emerge forth to fruition has no influence upon him. There is something of the same strength behind the true regional movement. It springs from the earth, a familiar geographical background, it is fashioned and expressed by craftsmanship and other creative faculties. It grows in the open, part of a pattern—is not lost among the monstrous maze of a machine age.

But if it is not to be so lost, swamped by the world's "passion for huge units", we must work hard and with courage to defend and develop, to intensify and enrich, to nurture into full bloom— Britain's regional renaissance.

INDEX